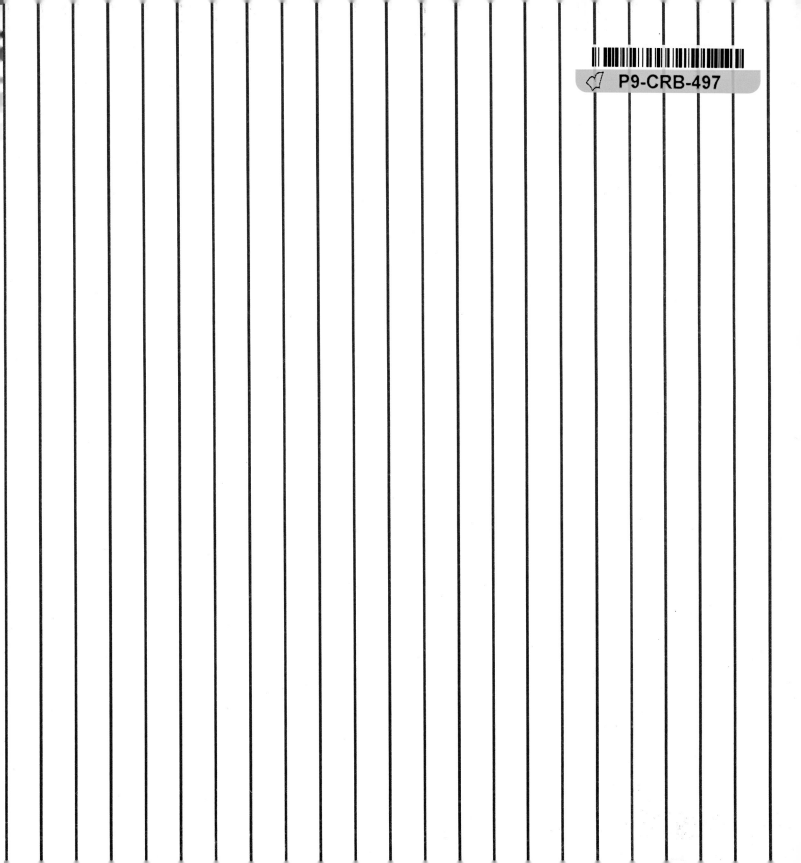

THE BRONX BOMBERS

**MEMORIES AND
MEMORABILIA OF
THE NEW YORK YANKEES**

Text by Bruce Chadwick
Photography by David M. Spindel

ABBEVILLE PRESS · PUBLISHERS
New York · London · Paris

To Margie and Rory.

—B.C.

To the inspirational spirits of Solomon Rappaport and Jacob Spindel.

—D.S.

What American magazine *didn't* have Joe D. on its cover?

Pages 2–3: 1927 Yankees (see p. 38). Frontispiece: A century of Yankee memorabilia. Title page: Babe Ruth doll and lighter. Contents, clockwise from left: banners (see p. 120), Ruth bust with signed ball, ticket to Gehrig memorial (see p. 41), '79 button (see p. 109), 1936 Yanks-Giants World Series program, Yankee clock (see p. 119), Mantle bean-bag game (see p. 94), Berra card (see p. 84).

EDITOR: Constance Herndon
PRODUCTION EDITORS: Robin James and Philip Reynolds
DESIGNER: Patricia Fabricant
PRODUCTION SUPERVISOR: Hope Koturo

Library of Congress Cataloging-in-Publication Data
Chadwick, Bruce.
   The Bronx Bombers: memories and memorabilia of the New York Yankees/by Bruce Chadwick: photography by David Spindel.
      p.   cm.
   Includes bibliographical references and index.
   ISBN 1-55859-243-1
   1. New York Yankees (Baseball team)—History.   I. Title.
GV875.N4C48   1991
796.357'64'097471—dc20   91-32026
                                 CIP

ACKNOWLEDGMENTS

We'd like to thank all the collectors, fans, and dealers, both kids and adults, who talked to us about their sports collections and let us take photos at the stores, museums, and baseball card shows we visited. In particular, we're grateful to Frank Palmer and Tony Marcello of New Jersey, who let us come into their homes to take photographs of their memorabilia. Thanks also to Josh Evans, president of Lelands, the New York sports auction house, who helped us locate and photograph several collections.

In addition we would also like to thank the athletes, sports personalities, and broadcasters who talked to us, particularly Mickey Mantle, Yogi Berra, Mel Allen, Willie Randolph, Ralph Terry, Reggie Jackson, Ron Guidry, Roberto Kelly, and Stump Merrill.

Finally, our special thanks to Constance Herndon, our editor, and Patricia Fabricant, our designer, who worked with us to turn a good book into a great one.

BRUCE CHADWICK AND DAVID SPINDEL

CONTENTS

ACKNOWLEDGMENTS • 7

INTRODUCTION
Pinstripes • 11

CHAPTER ONE
The Early Years
1904–1920 • 15

CHAPTER TWO
The Golden Age
1920–1935 • 23

CHAPTER THREE
The Yankee Clipper Arrives
1935–1949 • 43

CHAPTER FOUR
The Dynasty
1949–1960 • 59

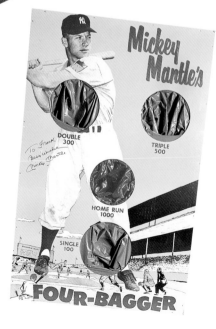

CHAPTER FIVE
After Casey
1960–1973 · 79

CHAPTER SIX
Steinbrenner and the Modern Age
1973–1978 · 97

CHAPTER SEVEN
Tomorrow's Team
1980s and On · III

YANKEE GREATS · 124

YANKEE STATS · 130

AUTOGRAPH PAGES · 134

BIBLIOGRAPHY · 136

INDEX · 137

PINSTRIPES

When my father was a little boy in the summer of 1927, the year Babe Ruth hit sixty home runs, he and his friends used to sneak away to Yankee Stadium in the afternoons. They paid their fifty cents, almost all in nickels, and got themselves the very choicest seats in the bleachers. The kids would race down to the rail when the Babe would take the outfield and yell to him.

"Hi Babe!" my father would yell at the top of his lungs, so that the legend would hear him call out over all those miles and miles of lush, green, sunlit outfield lawn. And Ruth would turn around, as he always did at the sound of a little boy's voice, wave his glove at the bleachers, smile, and yell back loudly, "Hiya, Kid!"

Years later, at the end of World War II, my father returned to the U.S. on a troop ship with hundreds of other GIs. One soldier from Texas told him proudly, "I'm just a farmer and now I've seen England, France, Italy. I've seen the king and queen, met Ike, and shook hands with Roosevelt. I've seen it all."

But my father smiled at him. "You've seen nothing," he said. "You never saw Babe Ruth hit a home run. I have. *I've* seen it all."

Over the years Yankee followers have seen just about everything a

That's really Gil McDougald's Yankee bag in the back, but the Ruth, DiMaggio, and Mantle jerseys are contemporary souvenirs.

The Yankees live forever in bubble gum cards. A Goudey Company card of Ruth, like that at top right, is worth $3,000 in great condition.

fan could dream up, for there has never been a baseball team, or any sports team, like the Yankees. The Bronx Bombers have not only had some of the best teams in baseball history, they've had them generation after generation. The Yankees dominated baseball in the '20s and '30s with Ruth and Gehrig, from the late '30s to early '50s with DiMaggio, and throughout the '50s and into the early '60s with Mantle, Ford, and manager Stengel. They stumbled in the '60s but came right back in the late '70s with Reggie Jackson, manager Billy Martin, and others. Even today, fol-

lowing nearly a dozen lackluster years, the tradition is so great that fans expect and even demand the team's return to glory.

The Yankees have won thirty-three pennants and twenty-two World Series championships. Twenty players, managers, and executives who spent most of their careers with the Yankees are now in the Hall of Fame. Yankee Stadium is the most famous field in the world, and the team has drawn record crowds even in last place.

The Yankees have been so good over the years that there developed a rare breed called the Yankee Hater, fans who despised them just because they were so good. The Dodgers were the beloved blue-collar team, the Giants were the tradition-laden team, the Red Sox were jinxed, the Cubs were unrequited, the Orioles were unfulfilled. But the Yankee Haters saw the Bronx Bombers as the too-smooth pinstriped executives of baseball, always winning and always winning big. "I'm a Cub fan, but I go over to the White Sox when the Yankees are in town," said one Chicago fan. "I go to see the Yankees lose."

The Yankees have been soaked in glory with the heroics of players like Babe Ruth, Mickey Mantle, and Joe DiMaggio. They have been steeped in tragedy with the deaths of Lou Gehrig and Thurman Munson. They have had lightning rods of

This sterling silver humidor given to Joe DiMaggio by his teammates at the conclusion of his fifty-six-game hitting streak is one of his prize possessions and one of the few on display in his San Francisco home. The ball was signed for DiMaggio by Ronald Reagan and Mikhail Gorbachev at a state dinner honoring the Soviet president; Gorbachev had specifically requested Joltin' Joe's presence at the dinner, and on being introduced, he and Reagan both pulled out balls for Joe to sign.

controversy like Reggie Jackson and George Steinbrenner, and home-spun teddy bears like Phil Rizzuto. They have had wits like Casey Stengel, intellects like Dr. Bobby Brown, and they've even had two guys who traded wives (Fritz Peterson and Mike Kekich in the '70s).

Finally, the Bombers have had and continue to have greatness. Ruth. Gehrig. DiMaggio. Lazzeri. Berra. Mantle. Ford. Jackson. Guidry. Mattingly. The Yankees have retired five times as many numbers as most other teams—indeed the team has had so many superstars that it had to build a monument park just to honor them all.

But the real greatness of the Yankees, the real fun in following them, was never who starred last but who will star next. That's exactly the feeling in New York now. Which of the hot young pitchers on a team roaring with promise will be the next Whitey Ford, which of the raw rookie sluggers will be the next Mickey Mantle? And where will that next World Series flag go?

CHAPTER ONE

THE EARLY YEARS

1904–1920

No team in American sports history has the legend, glory, and tradition of the New York Yankees, so it's hard to believe that the fabled Bronx Bombers were born in a rickety old sixteen-thousand-seat wooden stadium in the Washington Heights section of Manhattan, a stadium called Hilltop Park for no other reason than it was on the top of a hill. And the original Yankees were called the Highlanders, of all things, because they played on high land and a famous British military unit of the era was called Gordon's Highlanders.

It was there at Hilltop Park that the team's first owners, a political ward heeler named Big Bill Devery and a gambler named Frank Farrel, opened the franchise they purchased from the American League, which desperately needed a team in the nation's largest city. New York already had not one but two National League clubs, the Giants and the Robins (later to be called the Dodgers). Managed by Clark Griffith and led by Wee Willie Keeler (who hit .318), the Highlanders took the field in 1903 and finished fourth.

New York was a thriving baseball town at the turn of the century. The first organized baseball game ever played had taken place between two New York teams in Hoboken, New Jersey, in 1845, and by the mid-1870s over one hundred amateur teams played in organized leagues in

The start of the tradition—the New York Highlanders, 1909.

New York, some drawing over five thousand people per game. All Black teams played in the area as early as 1862 and in 1906 a Black professional team was launched. Nationwide there was such a thirst for baseball that in 1876 the National League was formed, including a New York team called the Mutuals. They folded after a year, but in 1884 the Giants joined and in 1890 so did a team from Brooklyn.

From 1890, when the great wave of immigration began, through 1910, New York was the fastest growing city in the world. The city was huge, getting bigger, and its appetite for baseball was enormous. The Dodgers of Brooklyn and the Giants of Manhattan won championships and pulled capacity crowds, a fact not lost on the American League, but the question remained—if some major American cities couldn't support *one* professional team, could New York support *three*? And could it support an American League franchise just blocks away from a National League team, the Giants?

It could.

The Highlanders and a local fan at spring training at Gray, Georgia, in 1908.

The Yankees were originally called the Highlanders. Their very first ballpark was a 16,000-seat temple of wooden grandstands and outfield advertising boards called Hilltop Park, in the Washington Heights section of Manhattan—a far cry from the Yankee Stadium to come. The team opened there in 1903 and finished fourth that year in the newly formed American League.

17

The mercurial Jack Chesbro became the only pitcher in baseball to win forty games in a season when he took forty-one in 1904. Despite his performance he was unable to win the final game of the season, which decided the pennant.

Success on the field and at the box office came early for the Highlanders, but left just as quickly. In 1904, behind the record-setting pitching of Jack Chesbro, who won forty-one games, the Highlanders finished second, just one game out of first. Ironically, Chesbro's forty-one wins meant little to his fans because a wild pitch in the final game lost the pennant. Fans, who were starting to like this brash new team, expected big things in 1905, but the team plunged to sixth place and did not contend for the pennant again until the Roaring Twenties.

Fans said the problem was not the team, but the meddling of the owners (sound familiar?). Unhappy with the team's performance, Devery and Farrel fired Griffith at the end of the 1907 season and replaced him with Kid Elberfeld. The Kid, a good player but a lousy manager, led the Highlanders to the basement and was canned. The owners then sacked the general manager and half the front office, and took over the operations themselves, hiring George Stallings as manager in 1909 and firing him in 1911. The 1912 season saw the arrival and departure of Harry Wolverton. Then there was Frank Chance, the great Cubs first baseman who was the end of Tinkers-to-Evers-to-Chance, the great double play combination. Finished with playing, he was eager to manage, but

after a year in New York, he was eager to manage somewhere else. He was followed by player-manager Roger Peckinpaugh, who was only twenty-three.

Devery and Farrel were doing as badly off the field as they were on it, both having reached the brink of financial ruin in different business ventures. Fed up with the Highlanders, they decided to sell the ball club in 1915. The new owners would change the face of baseball forever. Colonel Jacob Ruppert, a former congressman worth $75 million who owned one of the world's largest breweries, Ruppert Brewery, teamed up with construction millionaire Tillinghast Huston to purchase the club for an incredible $460,000 from the men who originally bought it for a mere $18,000.

Ruppert, a colonel in the Seventh Regiment of the National Guard, had served four terms in the U.S. Congress and was one of America's wealthiest and innovative businessmen. (It was Ruppert who designed the team's brand-new pinstriped uniform in the 1920s, using pinstripes because he thought the look would make the ever-growing Babe Ruth look slim.)

The team's wealthy new owners knew that it takes three things to build a great team—money, money, and money—and they had plenty of it. In 1915 they bought the contract of Frank "Home Run"

Beer baron Jacob Ruppert, whose money made it possible for the Yankees to buy the players they needed (thanks mostly to the good people of Boston), and whose purchases transformed the team into one of the dominant sports franchises of the Roaring Twenties.

The first great Yankee manager was Miller Huggins, the diminutive field boss who led the team to six pennants and three World Series.

20

Baker, a giant of the game, along with those of other players, and three years later they hired manager Miller Huggins away from the Saint Louis Cardinals to give the team stability as it climbed all the way to third place.

Around 1916 both fans and sportswriters, inspired perhaps by the red, white, and blue flags that seemed to fly everywhere at Hilltop, stopped calling the club the Highlanders and started calling it the New York Yankees. And not long after they moved out of Hilltop to share the Polo Grounds with the Giants, who were not happy about it. During these years the first pieces of memorabilia, scorecards, photographs, and ticket stubs began to circulate. And during these years the team was routinely demolished by the powerhouse Boston Red Sox, who dominated the league with stars like Harry Hooper, "Bullet" Joe Bush, and the talented young pitcher-slugger Babe Ruth.

What annoyed Ruppert and Yankee fans most were the Giants and the Dodgers. The Giants had been on the scene since 1884 and had built a dynasty, winning pennants in 1904 and 1905, the World Series in 1905, and more pennants in 1911, 1912, and 1913. For their part the Dodgers won pennants in 1899, 1900, 1916, and 1920. New York was a home of champions, everywhere but in Hilltop

Park. The other local teams were not only the best in the city, but the best in the country. And the Giants especially gnawed at Ruppert and his Yankees. After Hilltop burned down, the Yankees leased and shared the Polo Grounds with the Giants, but they were always the poor relations. The Giants continued to win pennants and boasted legendary stars like Christy Mathewson, Mike Donlin, and Joe McGinnity. The Giants had the country's greatest manager, John McGraw, their players always wound up in the nightlife columns, and they drew all the showgirls from Broadway plays to their games. The Yankees wanted a championship badly.

In 1918 the Yankees had a new manager, a new home, new owners, and a half-dozen solid new ballplayers. As the Roaring Twenties approached they seemed poised for greatness, but they needed one more ingredient—a genuine superstar. In the sale of the century, the sale that made the Yankees and ruined the Red Sox, Boston owner Harry Frazee sold Babe Ruth to the Yankees in 1919 for $100,000 and used the proceeds to finance Broadway plays. The Babe, who had smashed a record-breaking twenty-nine homers in 1919, was about to lead the Yankees into the golden age of baseball.

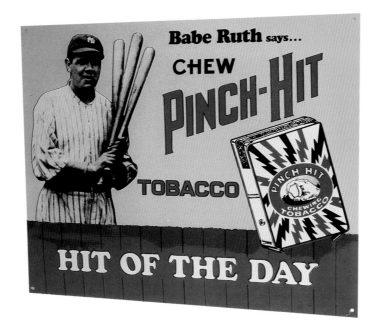

Pinch-Hit Chew— the tobacco of choice for America's greatest slugger.

21

THE GOLDEN AGE
1920–1935

he Roaring Twenties were the glory years in American sports. That single decade spawned some of the greatest legends of all time: in football, Knute Rockne and his Fighting Irish at Notre Dame; in tennis, big Bill Tilden; in boxing, Jack Dempsey; and in baseball, Babe Ruth, a big, sprawling, roaring bear of a man who could electrify sixty thousand people with one swat of his bat. Ruth was a man much larger than life, as large as the Roaring Twenties themselves. And what better place for him in the '20s than New York City, a town as wild and carefree as he was, a town with twenty daily newspapers just waiting to splatter his name all over their pages? It was a town crazy for baseball and a town craving a single great superstar. Ruth was it.

"You just can't imagine the kind of guy he was without seeing him play," teammate Lefty Gomez said years later. "He was a circus, a play, a movie, all rolled into one. Kids adored him. Men idolized him. Women loved him. There was something about him, something with men like that who come along once in a while, that made him great."

The Babe was a fan's delight. He'd come to the ballpark an hour before anyone else just to sign autographs and he'd go anywhere to see a sick kid. A recently uncovered photographer's assignment book lists appearances by Ruth at three different hospitals in one day—and in

The classic Ruth swing with the classic deep grandstand results.

23

This group of old programs is highlighted by one from the Yankees-Giants battle of 1922 (won by the Giants).

best pitchers in the history of the game, posting a 94–46 career record, with 23 wins and a 1.75 ERA in 1916 alone. His record of 29⅔ scoreless World Series innings stood for forty-three years.

But it was the home run that made Babe Ruth the most famous man in the country. People didn't come to see Ruth pitch or hit long singles or steal bases, they came to see him hit home runs, and he didn't disappoint. He set every home-run record there was, and then broke his own records again and again: 714 lifetime, 60 in one year (1927), and three in a single World Series game.

Everything about Ruth was mythical. He was a giant of a man—6 feet, 2 inches, 215 pounds—in an age when the average man was about 5 feet, 5 inches, 145 pounds. His body had an odd shape to it, with oversized arms and hands, a big pot belly, and thin, spindly legs. His bat weighed in at 44 ounces, the biggest in the majors. And his home-run swing was a three-act play in itself: when he'd miss, his whole body would swing around and you could hear him grunt thirty yards away.

He hit the kind of home runs fiction writers dreamed of. When Yankee Stadium opened in 1923, he hit a home run to inaugurate it. When a dying boy named Johnny Sylvester asked him to hit a home run for him, the Babe went out and hit not

between he played a ball game. He was also a hopeless night owl. When asked what it was like to be the Babe's roommate, Yankees outfielder Ping Bodie said, "I don't room with Babe Ruth . . . I room with his suitcase."

Everything Ruth did was bigger and better than anybody else. He hit an amazing .342 lifetime, with 2,873 hits, 1,356 extra base hits, and 2,211 RBIs. He played in ten World Series and even stole 123 bases (two in one World Series game). People forget that he was also one of the

Ruth surrounded by the usual gang of kids. The Babe loved children and children loved him. An old *New York Daily News* photographers' log, c. 1928, shows him visiting sick kids at three different hospitals in one day—and playing a game in between.

Most boys couldn't get World Series press pins (far left, from 1927) but they could join Esso's Babe Ruth Boys Club.

Ruth and admirers.

Signed picture of Ruth from 1924.

A copy of Ruth's will.

The Babe's chunky face adorned everything from key chains to watches in the '20s.

Below, one collector specializes in Ruth bats from the mid-'30s, including these three gems with a signed ball.

THE BABE

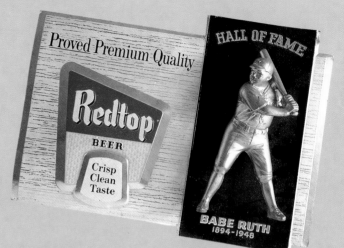

Ruth advertising one of his favorite hobbies. A sportswriter once said of him: "Forget the home runs. I once saw him down a huge mug of beer in a single gulp. . . ."

I saw Babe Ruth play dozens of times as a kid. When he hit one out it wasn't a home run, it was an event. Everybody would stand up and cheer and clap and stomp their feet as the ball went up and out. Ruth would trot around the bases very closely, his big body rocking back and forth on those spindly little legs of his. During the whole trip around the bases he would wave at fans and exchange chatter with the other team on the field. He would look at the fans as he went around the bases, and I swear you'd think he was looking right at you and waving right at you—60,000 people would feel like that. And celebrities were always at the Stadium. Bill "Bojangles" Robinson, the great dancer, would sit behind the Yankee dugout with Tom Mix, the cowboy movie star. Robinson would jump on the dugout roof when the Babe hit a home run and tap dance the entire time he circled the bases. Mix had this big cowboy hat and he'd wave it back and forth at the crowd as the Babe ran around. It was a show, the greatest show on earth.

—TONY MARCELLO, of Boonton, New Jersey

Babe Ruth signed more balls than he hit. Here on the left is a 1928 Yankee team ball and on the right, a glorious single signature by the Bambino.

one but two (and, somehow, the boy lived). He hit the "called shot" home run in the 1932 World Series. In his very last game as a player, he didn't give the fans a fond farewell home run—he socked *three* of them.

In 1928 Ruth was being paid $80,000, more than President Coolidge. When asked if he deserved more than the president, he quipped, "I had a better year."

But the most important thing about Ruth is that he arrived in New York in the spring of 1920 and promptly smashed fifty-four home runs the year after the "Black Sox" World Series scandal. If Ruth and his thunder had not arrived that year, and in media-mad New York, baseball, so badly tarnished, might not have survived.

With Ruth in his lineup, manager Miller Huggins built a dynasty and built it fast—aided by the wallet of Jacob Ruppert. The owner, his appetite whetted by the purchase of Ruth, went back to the Red Sox the following season and bought most of the team's stellar pitching staff. With deals that made New Yorkers happy and Bostonians cringe, Ruppert brought "Bullet" Joe Bush, Herb Pennock, and Waite Hoyt to New York. The Red Sox were so depleted by 1922 that they floundered in last place.

But it wasn't pitching that made the Yankees the terrors of the American

The general manager, check signer, and architect of the Yankee dynasty of the 1920s was Ed Barrow, who developed a strong farm system, traded for key Red Sox players including Ruth, and brought organization to a chaotic club. Under him, the Yanks won fourteen pennants and ten World Series.

A young Lou Gehrig gets his man in spring training.

League in the Roaring Twenties, it was a devastating lineup of sluggers, the legendary "Murderers Row." In addition to Ruth, Huggins could pencil into his lineup card Tony "Poosh 'em up" Lazzeri, who once hit sixty home runs in the minors and had seven 100-RBI seasons for the Yankees. Huggins had Bob Meusel, a 6 feet, 3 inch giant who pounded home runs whenever Ruth was quiet, once had 138 RBIs, and hit .309 lifetime. And then there was Mark Koenig, who hit .319 in 1928 and .500 in the '27 Series. These players and others

helped Huggins win pennants in 1921, 1922, and 1923, a World Series in '23, and more pennants in '26, '27, '28, '29, and '32 along with three more World Series. But more than anyone else, Huggins had home-grown Lou Gehrig.

Gehrig, the Iron Horse who played in a record 2,130 consecutive games, was always overshadowed by Ruth. He was the Avis to Ruth's Hertz so many times that people forget that in 1927, the year Ruth hit sixty home runs, Gehrig led him in homers on September 1, forty-six to forty-

The Babe entertaining the usually taciturn Lou Gehrig with some musical selections.

Gehrig's farewell speech was included on this recording of *The Greatest Moments in Sports,* featuring a cover picture of Ruth hugging the Iron Horse. Ordinarily, the wildly dissimilar men had a rather strained relationship.

three. Gehrig was a quiet, happily married man whose idea of a wild weekend was reading magazines with his wife and mother. He was shy, and hid from the press and public whenever he could. Indeed today a Gehrig autograph is worth more than a Ruth because Ruth signed everything and Gehrig practically nothing. One woman, who played pickup baseball with Gehrig in Central Park when he was at Columbia, tells this story:

"We knew he was a great one, and we kept asking him to autograph stuff for us after games and he kept refusing. . . . Finally, you know what we had to do to get the autographs? We got chains and tied up his car and hold him we wouldn't undo

it unless he signed stuff for us. He did, and he drove home," she said.

New Yorkers came to love the mild-mannered Gehrig dearly, but in a very different way than they loved Ruth, the all-night carouser who thrived in the media spotlight. Gehrig was the strong, sturdy, productive player who anchored the Yankees, while Ruth was the star. The two men were dramatic opposites and, as one might expect, theirs was a strained relationship (at one point Ruth allegedly offended some friends of Gehrig's and Lou took it personally).

Gehrig was a native New Yorker who set all kinds of college records at Columbia with a .444 average. Like the

Above, Lou Gehrig, always second banana to the flamboyant Ruth, finished his extraordinary **career with 493 homeruns. When he died at thirty-seven, a nation mourned.** **Right, this remarkable collection of Lou Gehrig material chronicles the career of the slugger.**

young Ruth, he could pitch as well as hit, fanning seventeen in one game, and like Ruth he was huge, a 6 feet, 2 inch, 200 pounder with big hands and an easy, powerful, unbelievably level swing. A graceful first baseman with a feel for where the ball was going, he seemed to turn his heavy body into elastic as he stretched for the ball at first.

The Iron Horse came up to the majors for good in 1925, one day replacing Wally Pipp, who had a headache. He hit .295 that first year with twenty homers and continued to shine, hitting another forty-seven in 1927 only to be over-shadowed by Ruth's sixty. Numbers tell the amazing story of Gehrig: he had 184 RBIs in 1931, a record that still stands; he had 100 or more RBIs and runs in every full season he played; he hit 493 home runs (becoming the first man in this century to hit four homers in one game), 1,990 RBIs, and averaged .340 lifetime.

The one-two punch of Ruth and Gehrig, with good hitters in front and behind them, made the Yankees nearly invincible in the Roaring Twenties. They were the greatest dynasty in sports, and their fans loved them. Indeed so many Yankee fans flooded the Polo Grounds from 1920 to 1922 that Ruppert had to build Yankee Stadium, the "House That Ruth Built," just

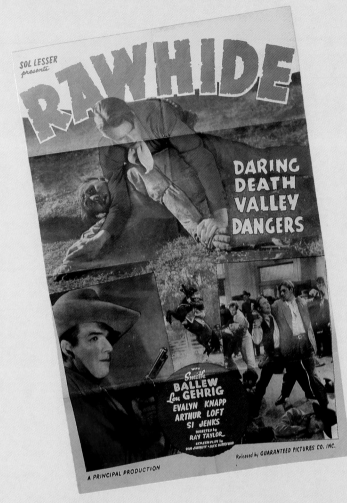

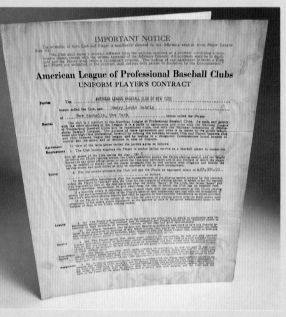

According to the
terms of this player's
contract, Lou Gehrig
was paid $23,000 in
1933. The contract
itself recently sold
for more than that.

Someone convinced
Lou Gehrig to take a
part in a film called
Rawhide in the '30s,
a performance that
inspired one critic
to write that as an
actor, Lou was a very
good first baseman.

Kids in the '20s
joined Lou Gehrig's
Knot Hole Gang.

The House That Ruth Built: Yankee Stadium on opening day in 1923. Appropriately, the Babe hit a home run in the very first game.

to hold them all. It was in the 1920s, too, when the thin "strip" baseball cards appeared and became popular with kids, as did team-autographed baseballs. The Yankees were so good that a distinctive new Yankee fan emerged, a fan who was used to success and demanded more of it. The World Series, not falling leaves, marked October on the Yankee fans' calendar.

The Yankees, with Ruth, Gehrig, and the others, became more than a baseball team, they became a show—the biggest

show in all of sports. In 1920, Ruth's first year in New York, the Yankees drew 1.3 million fans to the Polo Grounds—not only a record but twice what any other team in baseball drew that year. By the late '20s, they were attracting over two million fans a year at home. On the road, Yankee drawing power was as fearsome as Yankee bats. Attendance at many parks would double and triple when Ruth, Gehrig & Company came to town. In the off-season, too, the Yanks were number one,

Companies would take out colorful newspaper ads like this one to sell such commemorative material as the accompanying bat, balls, and hat.

Big Babe, along with a handsome old clock and a patch.

In the early 1960s, producers reissued 1920s film and made fifteen-minute Ruth adventures like this one, which featured the King of Swat in a short entitled *Perfect Control*. In most others the great Ruth cavorted with little kids.

as Ruth and Gehrig frequently led barnstorming teams across America after the season ended, drawing sellout crowds.

The highlight of the '20s for the Yankees came in 1927, although for any other team it would have been the highlight of its history. "Everything meshed for us—the personalities, the manager, the luck, everything," said Mark Koenig. The Yanks' '27 team, said to be the greatest ever to play baseball, featured twenty-game winner Hoyt and three more pitchers who won eighteen or more. The team batting average reached a startling .307. That's right . . . the team average. It was the wondrous year in which Ruth and Gehrig battled for the home-run championship of the century, with Gehrig actually leading Ruth by one home run going into the last month of the season. Ruth wound up with an amazing sixty, a mark not to be topped for thirty-four years, while Gehrig hit forty-seven for good measure, averaging .373 and hitting 175 RBIs. Tony Lazzeri hit .309 but only posted the sixth-highest average on the club. The team led the league from the first day of the season to the last, winning 110 games and taking the pennant by

Poster from the 1927 Series, Yanks vs. Pittsburgh.

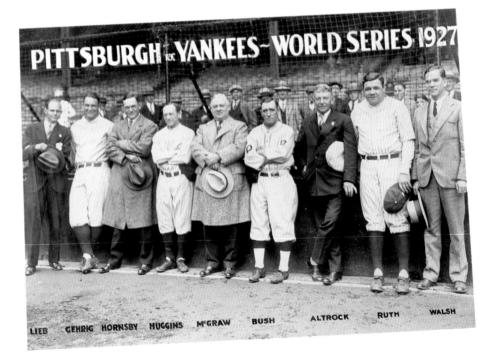

The 1927 Yankees, led by Babe Ruth, Lou Gehrig, and the legendary "Murderers Row," was perhaps the most powerful baseball team to ever take the field. The four starting pitchers won eighteen games or more and the team batting average was a stunning .307.

nineteen. They swept Pittsburgh 4–0 in the World Series, with many claiming that the Pirates gave up before the first game after watching the Yanks take batting practice. During that momentous warmup, legend has it, Gehrig hit ten home runs, followed by Ruth who hit another ten followed by an eleventh that sailed clear out of the park.

The Yanks won it all again in 1928, but then lost the pennant to Connie Mack and his Philadelphia Athletics each of the

next three years. They bounced back under new manager Joe McCarthy in 1932 to take the world championship again. Between 1936 and 1943 they won the pennant in seven of eight years and took the Series in six of seven.

It was a heady time for New York fans, who traveled back and forth to the stadium in the Bronx by car and (mostly) subway (what fan can forget the El running behind the bullpen in right field?). They had a great team playing great baseball over

39

Stricken by a fatal blood disease now known as Lou Gehrig's Disease, the Iron Horse bows his head during a farewell speech at Yankee Stadium, July 4, 1939.

the course of an entire generation. Men and women who saw the Yanks in the World Series in 1921 were now parents taking their own children to see their beloved Yankees in other World Series. And those kids, of course, would bring their own kids to see the Yanks in the '50s Series. Spanning a generation of New

Yorkers and looking toward a new one, the dynasty was complete.

But a dark cloud appeared over Yankee Stadium at the end of the 1930s. After playing in 2,130 consecutive games, a record of courage and endurance that may never be equaled, Lou Gehrig, the Iron Horse, was dying. He had a rare blood dis-

Shortly after his death in 1941 the Yankees held a memorial game for Lou Gehrig—on the Fourth of July—and issued these gorgeous tickets for it. One woman who was there that day swears every one of the 67,000 fans cried.

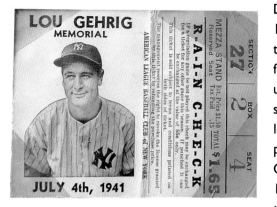

LOU GEHRIG
MEMORIAL

JULY 4th, 1941

Gary Cooper played Lou Gehrig in *The Pride of the Yankees,* the best sports movie ever made. During World War II when Cooper toured USO camps in Europe, soldiers would always ask him to recite Gehrig's farewell speech (". . . I consider myself the luckiest man on the face of the earth . . ."), a soliloquy that brought tears to the GIs and, after several dozen renditions, to Cooper too.

Day was held at Yankee Stadium on July 4, 1941, a month after Gehrig's death, and tickets from that day, with Gehrig's smiling face on them, are ringing memorabilia tributes to his greatness. His death added something very different to the growing legacy of the Yankees, too—courage and pain. In a terrible sense, the death of Lou Gehrig (and that of Thurman Munson in 1979) made the Yankee legend what it is today—a heroic legend of both triumph and tragedy.

order, now known as Lou Gehrig's Disease, and it was cutting him down in his prime. When his batting average dipped below .200 and he found himself struggling just to stand up on ground balls, Gehrig, the team captain, took himself out of the lineup in the spring of 1939. His last public appearance was on July 4, 1939, Lou Gehrig Day at Yankee Stadium. Once a huge hulk of a man, the powerhouse of a power lineup, Gehrig had begun to grow thin and weak. But in his memorable speech, seen by every kid in the country in the Gary Cooper movie *The Pride of the Yankees,* he never uttered a word of self-pity. Addressing the jammed stadium crowd, which he had thrilled so many times, the dying Gehrig declared, "Today, I consider myself the luckiest man on the face of the earth."

Two years later, Gehrig died at the age of thirty-seven. A Lou Gehrig Memorial

CHAPTER THREE

THE YANKEE CLIPPER ARRIVES

1935–1949

Even before Gehrig's death the changing of the Yankee guard had begun, most momentously in 1935 with the departure of Babe Ruth. He had wanted to manage the team, but the front office feared he would manage them like he managed himself, and they turned him down. The Babe then demanded to be traded to a club where he could eventually become manager, so the legend was let go and went to the Boston Braves. While he later coached with the Dodgers, he never became a manager and retired a bitter man.

You might think that the loss of the Babe would throw the Yanks into a tailspin, but it had little effect. As fate would have it, the year after Ruth left a skinny young kid named Joe DiMaggio arrived as a rookie. He was brand new to New York and brand new to baseball. He hadn't even played the game until he was seventeen years old but in a few short years he had become a West Coast legend, batting .398 in the Pacific Coast League and hitting safely in sixty-one straight games. The Yanks bought his contract for all of $25,000, which was probably a better deal than Peter Minuit got when he bought Manhattan from the Indians for $26.

After the Babe's departure the Yanks slipped to second in 1935, but the team was still a powerhouse. Gehrig continued to lead the lineup, which at that point featured Frank Crosetti, Tony Lazzeri, Red Rolfe,

Joe DiMaggio had one of the most graceful swings of all time. The elegant Yankee Clipper, a great gentleman on and off the field, hit .325 lifetime and made history with his incredible fifty-six-game hitting streak in 1941.

43

Lefty Gomez, great
pitcher and wit of
the Bronx Bombers.

George Selkirk, and Bill Dickey. The
mound staff was led by twenty-game-
winner Red Ruffing and by Lefty Gomez.
The team roared back in 1936 to win the
pennant, the first of four in a row, and
once again faced the cross-town Giants in
the World Series.

The '36 World Series was a perfect
example of what baseball was like for New
York and for the Yankees. The city dominated baseball in those days. If the Yankees
weren't winning pennants, the Dodgers or
Giants were, and often the teams faced
each other in the World Series, AKA the
"Subway Series." The Dodgers won pennants in 1890, 1899, 1900, 1916, and 1920.
The Giants won pennants in 1885, 1888,
1889, 1904, 1905, 1911, 1912, 1913, 1917,
1921, 1922, 1923, 1924, 1933, and 1936.
The Yankees didn't capture their first pennant until 1921, but their string went on to
include 1922, 1923, 1926, 1927, 1928,

Bill Dickey's cap rest-
ing on a first base
from the old Yankee
Stadium.

Bill Dickey was a truly great defensive catcher, catching a hundred or more games thirteen years in a row. He hit .300 in ten of his first eleven seasons.

Far right, one young fan cut out a *Boys' Life* page from 1928, "The Catcher and his Duties," and got Bill Dickey and Yogi Berra to sign it (below the fold).

Below, in the '20s and '30s the Yankees issued commemorative watches to celebrate World Series and pennants. The top watch belonged to owner Jacob Ruppert and the bottom to Lefty Gomez.

THE CATCHER AND HIS DUTIES

1932, 1936, 1937, 1938, and 1939. That's thirty-one pennants by a New York team out of fifty-five years, and twenty-six out of forty since the turn of the century. Pretty impressive.

Despite all those early pennants it wasn't until 1921 that two New York teams clashed in the World Series. That year the mighty Giants met the upstart Yankees and Babe Ruth, playing every game at the Polo Grounds because the stadium served as both teams' home field (the Yankees leased it from the Giants). The Yankees lost that one to their own landlords and the next year they fell once again to the Giants—primarily because John

McGraw's pitchers held Babe Ruth to only two hits. Both teams fumed about everything connected to same-field Series, even down to who would wear "away" uniforms, and that feuding started the tremendous Subway Series rivalry that would later include the Dodgers. Finally in 1923 the Yanks moved out of the Polo Grounds altogether and into shiny new Yankee Stadium. That year the rivalry hit its peak—and that year the Bombers first thrashed the Dodgers in the World Series, 4–1.

The Yankees and the Giants always had superstars, and that was true again in 1936 when the Yanks blazed into October with Gehrig having one of his finest years

45

Joe McCarthy managed the Yanks to nine pennants (four in a row from 1936 to 1939) and seven second-place finishes.

Pitcher Lefty Gomez signed this framed 1938 Yankees-Cubs program.

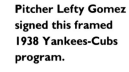

46

and a young Joe DiMaggio sizzling. The Giants were brilliant, too, led by screwball pitcher Carl Hubbell, who had posted a 26–6 record that year. He handcuffed the Yanks in game one, 6–1, but the Yankee locomotive woke up in game two and the pinstripers blasted the Giants, 18–4. The Giants never recovered and the Yanks took the Series four games to two. The team then went on to win pennants in seven of the next eight seasons and won the World Series six more times.

Over the next few years, the team continued to change. Gehrig died and Lazzeri and Rolfe left, replaced by tough

young stars who carried on the Yankee tradition. These men included Phil Rizzuto, who spent his entire life with the team as a player and then a broadcaster, Joe Gordon, one of the '40s' most consistent hitters, Tommy Henrich, Charlie "King Kong" Keller, and pitcher Spud Chandler. The Yankees were balanced, as always, with superior hitting, good fielding, and consistent pitching. In Joe McCarthy they had one of the game's great managers. Even though Ruth and Gehrig were gone, the fans turned out regularly to cheer the team. And, of course, there was Joltin' Joe DiMaggio.

Life on the field always seemed easy for DiMaggio. He never really made a great catch in center field because he got such a great jump on the ball that he was there before it was and caught the ball with an easy stride. He had the most graceful, effortless swing in the history of baseball, a long, easy swing from a thin body straddling wide-set feet.

"He had an unusual body," said broadcaster Mel Allen, who saw him play hundreds of times. "He had long arms, which enabled him to generate great bat speed and move quicker than most hitters. You couldn't blow anything by him or fool him because he was moving that bat a hundredth of a second faster than any other man. He had very long, slender legs which

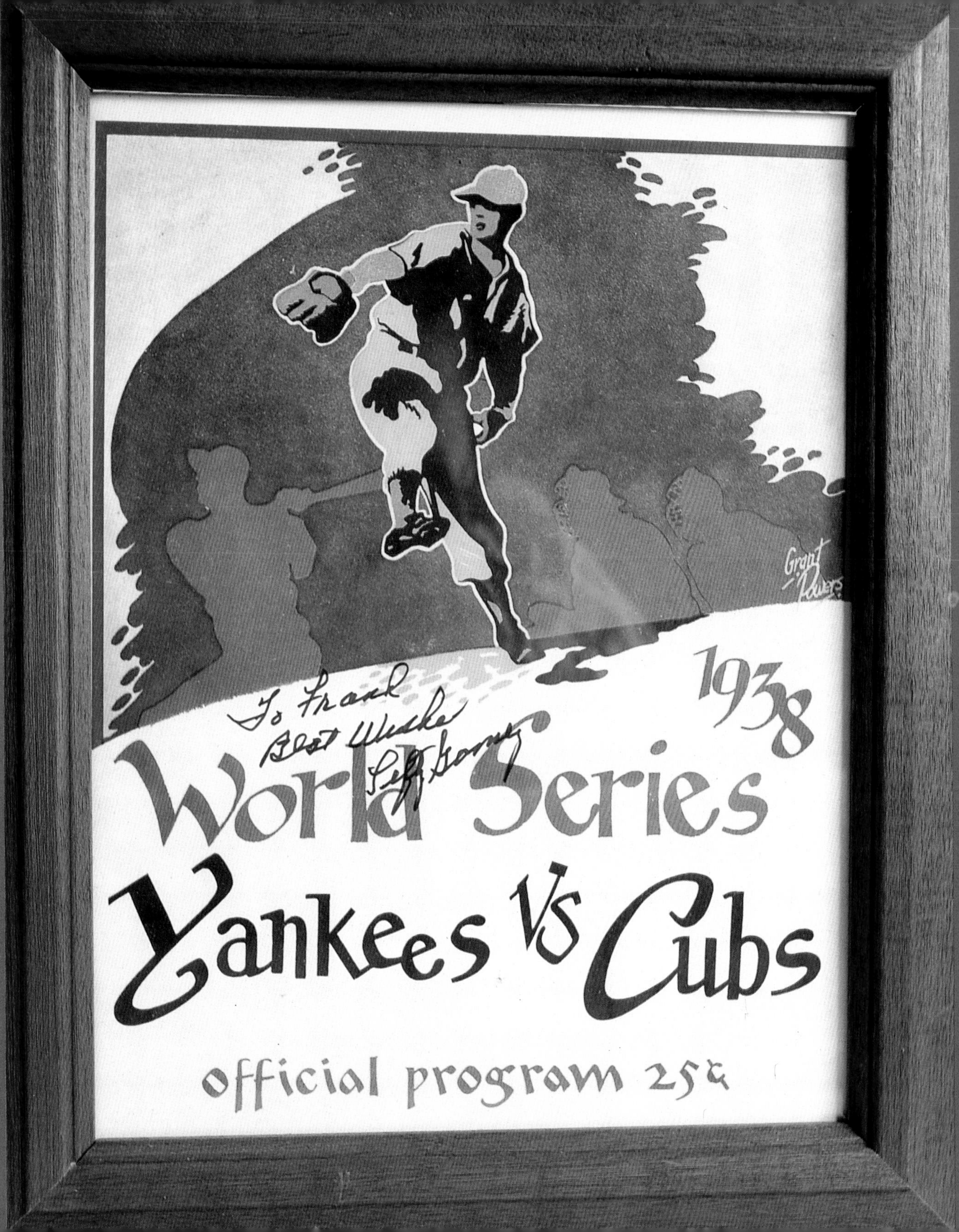
Grant Powers
To Frank
Best Wishes
Lefty Gomez
1938
World Series
Yankees vs Cubs
official program 25¢

Please admit bearer

to the center aisle of

Saint Patricks Cathedral

for the Funeral Service for

George Herman Ruth

A 1937 bronze clock devoted to the accomplishments of George Herman Ruth.

The Babe died in 1948 and following a wake at Yankee Stadium a privileged few were invited to his funeral at New York's Saint Patrick's Cathedral.

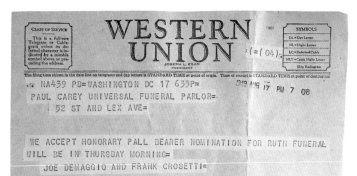

CLASS OF SERVICE

This is a full-rate Telegram or Cablegram unless its deferred character is indicated by a suitable symbol above or preceding the address.

WESTERN UNION

JOSEPH L. EGAN
PRESIDENT

SYMBOLS

DL=Day Letter

NL=Night Letter

LC=Deferred Cable

NLT=Cable Night Letter

Ship Radiogram

The filing time shown in the date line on telegrams and day letters is STANDARD TIME at point of origin. Time of receipt is STANDARD TIME at point of destination

NA439 PD=WASHINGTON DC 17 635P=   1948 AUG 19   PM 7 08

PAUL CAREY UNIVERSAL FUNERAL PARLOR=

52 ST AND LEX AVE=

WE ACCEPT HONORARY PALL BEARER NOMINATION FOR RUTH FUNERAL

WILL BE IN THURSDAY MORNING=

JOE DEMAGGIO AND FRANK CROSETTI=

THE COMPANY WILL APPRECIATE SUGGESTIONS FROM ITS PATRONS CONCERNING ITS SERVICE

Telegram with which Joe DiMaggio (spelled wrong) and Frank Crosetti agreed to serve as pallbearer at Ruth's funeral.

The Babe bidding adoring fans farewell in 1947. New York police feared a riot at a funeral-home wake the next year so the Babe was waked in Yankee Stadium itself and over 100,000 fans passed by his bier to pay final respects.

This DiMaggio collection has a matchbook from Joe's first restaurant in San Francisco, the city where he still lives.

This display of DiMaggio memorabilia includes rare sheet music from the wildly popular '40s song "Joltin' Joe DiMaggio."

enabled him to cover much more ground than any other man with lengthy strides. That cut down the time he needed to get to a place in the outfield.

"But I believe the secret to Joe was that mentally he had unbelievable instincts," continued Allen. "As soon as a ball was hit—no, before it was hit—he'd be moving. He just knew what was going to happen. The same with hitting. His arms and wrists would be moving the right way quicker than was possible. That's what made it all look so easy."

Phil Rizzuto never saw his teammate make a diving catch. "He'd just be there. You'd turn your head as a screeching line drive would be headed towards the alley between left and center and you knew, you just knew from years of experience, that it was going to the wall. By the time your head turned all the way around to follow, Joe would be there, just waiting for it, like you'd wait for a bus. I don't know how he got there, but he was there."

DiMaggio's Hall-of-Fame statistics are legendary. He hit .325 lifetime and .422 in World Series play. He slashed 361 home runs, 2,214 hits, and 1,537 RBIs. He was the best fielding outfielder of his era. Unlike any other reigning superstar, DiMaggio was a quiet, reclusive man who didn't enjoy small talk. He was not aloof from his teammates, but was silent most of

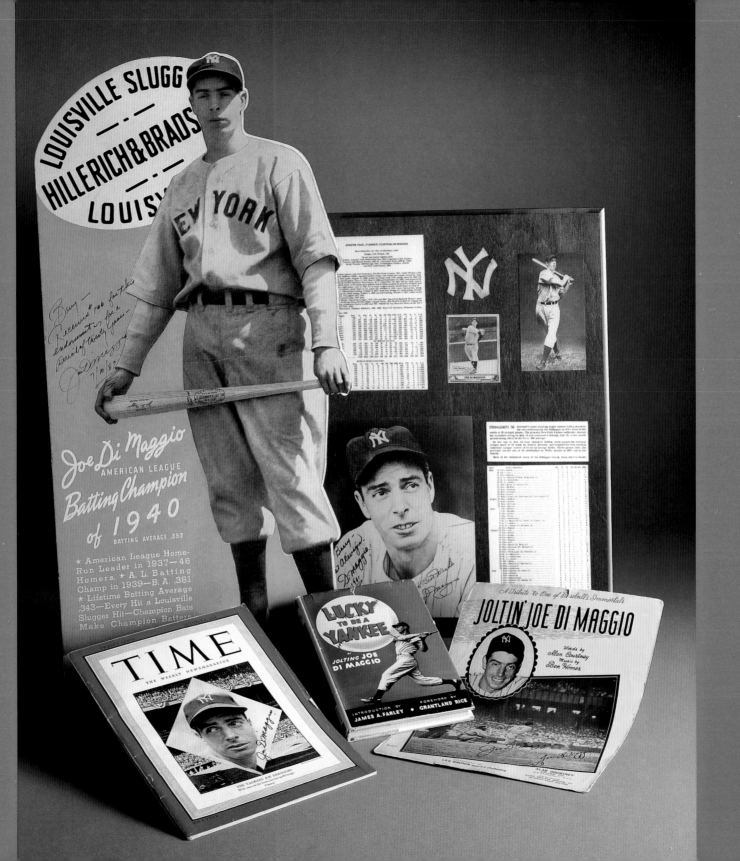

A rare personalized DiMaggio signature on a large-scale photo.

"It's really great! And makes as great a salad as I've ever tasted."

Joe DiMaggio

That's how the great Joe DiMaggio one of the newest members of baseball's "Hall of Fame", feels about Kraft's new Italian Dressing. Formerly a restaurateur, Joe knows a fine dressing when he tastes one.

● All you need do is make one salad with this golden, oil-and-vinegar dressing and we bet you'll agree. Kraft's new Italian dressing is *fabulously good!* Rare herbs, fresh spices and just the right touch of garlic give it a most delicious, unusual flavor. And the way it clings to the greens, so every bite *stays* coated, is a delight to behold. Better stop right now and put Kraft Italian on your shopping list.

KRAFT Italian dressing

NEW!

Kraft ITALIAN DRESSING

SEPTEMBER 18, 1955 parade 11

Like today's stars, DiMaggio was not reluctant to lend his name to advertising —here we see a Kraft salad dressing ad.

New Jersey collector Tony Marcello has saved over two hundred—odd license plates and reveres none more than these two, shown with a DiMaggio signed ball and two cards.

•NEW JERSEY•
YANKS 5
•GARDEN STATE•

•OCEAN STATE•
DIMAG-5
•RHODE ISLAND•

1839 1939
baseball Centennial

JOLTIN' JOE

A recording of "Joltin' Joe DiMaggio," played by Les Brown and his orchestra.

DiMaggio baseball cards are rare but in the '40s pictures and busts of the slugger were common. Note photo of the very little Joe at left front.

My first husband was a big Yankee fan. In the late '40s, early '50s, we lived a few blocks from the stadium and we'd walk over to the game. We saw maybe twenty or thirty games a year. We'd sit out in the bleachers and stare at Joe DiMaggio for three hours.

—DOROTHY BERGMAN of Manhattan

Fans love to collect commemorative items, like this hundredth anniversary of baseball World Series program and a Mickey Mantle Day banner.

there!" Everybody stopped. The veteran pulled back, Rizzuto jumped in, and he was never shut out again.

Dubbed the Yankee Clipper, DiMaggio became the most famous athlete in the country. He graced the cover of practically every magazine on the news-stands, married film star Marilyn Monroe, had a song written about him ("Joltin' Joe DiMaggio," recorded by Les Brown in 1941), and gained literary fame when Hemingway referred to him as "the great DiMaggio" in *The Old Man and the Sea*.

"He was a sharp dresser, a polite, helpful guy. He was first class all the way," said Mickey Mantle.

DiMaggio led the Yankees to four straight pennants and four straight world championships in '36, '37, '38, and '39. But even though Joe hit .352, the team slipped to third in 1940 and stumbled through the beginning of the 1941 season. Then, on May 15, DiMaggio began his fabled hitting streak. He hit safely in ten games, then twenty, then thirty, then forty. The news-papers had a field day, reporting every game, every hit, every pitch. He zeroed in on George Sisler's record forty-one-game streak only to find that reporters unearthed a little-known streak of forty-four games by Wee Willie Keeler way back in 1897. It really didn't matter. DiMaggio was so hot he was hitting .408.

the time. No loud bragging, no team pep talks, this was leadership by example. And when the poker-face DiMaggio did talk, everybody listened.

When Rizzuto was a rookie, he kept missing his turn in the batting cage as play-ers jumped in and out and DiMaggio watched from nearby. Rizzuto had missed eight turns and was frustrated. As his ninth turn came up and another veteran pre-pared to step in front of him, DiMaggio yelled out at the Scooter, "Rizzuto, get in

Above, Joltin' Joe, national hero.

Below, Yankee World Series ticket stubs from 1928 and 1947, when ticket prices went up from $5.50 to $8.00.

Sisler's record fell on June 29, and on July 2, to make sure there was no debate about it, he broke Keeler's record with a towering home run.

With the pressure off, Joe just kept steaming ahead like a brakeless train going downhill. The hits came easily and the streak went on and on. On July 17 the cabbie who drove DiMaggio to the park in Cleveland put the hex on him by telling him that the streak would end that night—and in front of a capacity crowd of 67,000 it finally did at fifty-six. What most people don't know, however, is that once the streak ended the Clipper immediately went on another sixteen-game hitting streak, ultimately hitting in seventy-two of seventy-three games. His streak remains today the most sacred of baseball records, one not even approached by Pete Rose, who came closest with forty-four.

Over the years many people have told me I should have wanted it to end, to end the pressure. I never wanted it to end. I wish it could have lasted all season. People forget that after I was stopped at fifty-six games, I then hit safely in seventeen more games. In the minors, I once hit in sixty-one straight games. I'm not looking for a pat on the back. I'm just saying that when you get in one of those things you never know how far they'll go.

—JOE DiMAGGIO, New York Yankees

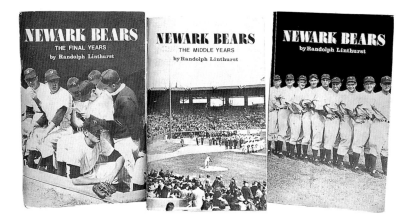

In the '30s the Newark Bears were the best minor-league team in the country,

maybe in history, sending dozens of Yankee greats up to the big club.

Joe DiMaggio was often compared to Ted Williams in those years. The two great Hall of Famers played against each other all year and their stats were Herculean. Because the Yanks and Red Sox were such rivals, comparisons of the two seemed natural. The team rivalry had begun back in 1919, when the Red Sox sold Ruth and other top stars to the Yankees. That move ruined the Red Sox, so devastating the franchise that the team went into deepfreeze, and New England fans never forgave Sox owner Harry Frazee. By the mid-'40s, however, the Sox were heating up again, even making it to the World Series in 1946. Boston lost to Cincinnati, but the Red Sox jinx really seemed to have gained strength in the late '40s as the Yankee–Red Sox rivalry grew.

The late '40s were a transition time for the Yankees. The best players had returned from World War II but others had retired, so young players were being brought up from the minors, particularly from the Newark Bears. The anchor for the post-war team was DiMaggio, as usual. Joe, who suffered many injuries fans never knew about, played through the 1951 season and then retired.

When asked years later what he was proudest of—the hitting streak or the home runs or the Hall of Fame selection—DiMaggio shook his head slowly.

Going to see the Newark Bears [the Yankees' farm team] was great fun. I lived a few miles from Ruppert Stadium and went down on a bus with my friends. In those days the minor leagues had a lot of good players from the majors on their way down as well as good players on their way up to the majors. So you saw teams with good players and a lot of names. I used to drive players crazy for autographs and eventually, to get rid of me, they started giving me uniforms if I didn't bother them for autographs. That got me started as a collector and as a fan.

—Collector BARRY HALPER of New Jersey

The most famous missed ball ever: Tommy Henrich swings and misses a third strike, but the pitch gets away from catcher Mickey Owen. At time, Dodgers held a 4–3 lead with two out in the ninth. Henrich went to first on the missed ball, DiMaggio then singled, Charlie Keller doubled, and the Yanks won the game, 7–4, followed by the Series.

"It wasn't the records, the Hall of Fame. It was none of that. I was most proud that I was a Yankee," he said.

Today, forty years after his retirement, the well-dressed, elegant, and articulate DiMaggio is still a much-sought speaker and the most popular guest at baseball card shows, besieged by kids and adults alike wherever he goes. In 1988, one-handed pitcher Jim Abbott was named All America, received the Sullivan Award as best amateur athlete, led his country to victory in the Olympics, and won dozens of other awards. When asked to name his greatest thrill, however, his eyes lit up and his voice rose with excitement as he answered, "I got to meet Joe DiMaggio."

Even for today's stars, the Yankee Clipper remains a legend.

World War II's drain on manpower made it possible for the obscure Ernie "Tiny" Bonham to be hailed by the press as a "Yankee pitching ace."

THE DYNASTY
1949–1960

Although the Yankees had dominated the major leagues during the '30s and '40s, the team didn't really become a dynasty, an invincible force, until the arrival in 1949 of an unlikely character named Charles Dillon Stengel, known to history as Casey. Already fifty-eight years old if not exactly over the hill, he brought baggage with him more fit for a vaudeville act than the nation's finest baseball team. He had an extra large set of ears on an extra large head on a body that always seemed smaller than its listed 5 feet, 11 inches. Stengel was a cartoon of a man, known best during his playing days for coming to bat and doffing his cap to reveal a bird under it. He also hit the first inside-the-park home run in a World Series game. He had played with mediocrity for just about every team in the majors, batting a respectable .284. As a manager he had been a disaster, leading Brooklyn to sixth, fifth, and seventh place finishes in three years there in the '30s before moving to Boston, where his clubs finished an inglorious fifth, sixth, and seventh during four years.

Fans, writers, and players regarded him first and foremost as a clown —which he certainly looked like, with that rubbery face, big ears, and a too-large uniform always dangling from his aging frame. And, of course, he certainly talked like one. The American public had never heard anyone talk like Casey, the "Ol' Perfessor" (he was, in fact, a college professor at

The Ol' Perfessor, Casey Stengel (believe it or not, he actually *was* once a full-time college professor). Casey had gained instant fame as a player when he got up to bat, doffed his cap, and a bird flew out. As the team's loquacious manager he became a baseball immortal, leading the Yanks to ten pennants and seven World Series in just twelve years.

59

Pennants from the early '50s.

against lefty Mel Parnell when they went to Boston. Right against left, correct? Plus Boston's big wall in left field was heaven to righties. The problem was, Parnell still killed the Yankees. Well, for the hell of it, Casey put in a lineup of all lefties. It was crazy. It was nuts. Parnell never beat the Yankees again.

"I remember one time Gene Woodling was hitting a ton," remembered Billy Martin. "It was the first inning. Casey sent in Hank Bauer to pinch hit for Gene. That had never been done, ever. He says, in that gravelly voice of his, 'Bauer, go in there and hit a home run.' Damned if Bauer didn't get up and hit one out. Casey had the wildest instinct I ever saw."

Casey's arrival transformed the Yankees. They took the pennant and the World Series in 1949 and promptly went on to dominate baseball as no team had dominated any sport. Casey's team won pennants and Series championships again in 1950, with the help of sensational rookie pitcher Whitey Ford, who went 9–1. DiMaggio retired in 1951, but up came strongman Mickey Mantle, the greatest slugger of his age and a man who put meat in the Yankee batting order. The team rolled to five pennants and five World Series championships in a row and took a total of ten pennants and seven World Series titles in the twelve years Casey held

one time). He spoke Stengelese, and while no one understood it, everyone loved it.

"Jerry Lumpe is the best hitter in baseball, until you put him in the lineup," he once cracked. When asked about platooning, he said, "What's the secret to platooning? There's not much to it. You put a right-hand hitter against a left-hand pitcher and a left-hand hitter against a right-hand pitcher and on cloudy days you use a fastball pitcher."

Don't shake your head too much. Nobody back in 1949 could figure it out either.

He did crazy things with the Yankee team. Everybody put in right-hand hitters

In the old days
crowds left Yankee
Stadium by walking
directly across the
field. Here, 67,000
leave a 1950 World
Series game via the
outfield.

61

Right, a 1960 program heralding Yankee greats of years gone by.

Below, the jersey of Johnny Mize, who played for the Yanks from 1949 to 1953 and led the league in pinch hitting for three of those seasons. Although Mize played most of his career with the Giants, "the Giant fans never forgave me for playing with the Yankees," he said years later.

forth. The Yankees had become such a dynasty that everywhere the cry went up, "Break up the Yankees!" They were virtually invincible, regarded so highly and envied by so many that *Damn Yankees,* a Broadway play and later a movie in which the help of the Devil was required to beat the team, became the hit of the day.

"Everybody wanted to beat the Yankees," declared Ed Charles, a Kansas City player in the '50s who went on to glory with the Mets. "Fans in other cities didn't

Yankees in first Stadium All-Star Game (July 11, 1939)

DI MAGGIO
CROSETTI
DICKEY
McCARTHY
ROLFE
MURPHY
GORDON
GOMEZ
SELKIRK
RUFFING

NEW YORK Yankees 1960

OFFICIAL PROGRAM AND SCORE CARD 15 CENTS

hate the Yankees. That's a myth. They were just awed by them. They were just too good. Charlie Finley, Kansas City's owner then, would walk through the locker room and smile at each player when we beat anybody else, but when we'd beat the Yankees, he'd hand each player a $100 bill. That's how much he wanted them."

Looking back, players on those great Yankee teams recognize that more than rivalry, luck, or Casey's magic drove in all those runs.

Left, this closetful of memorabilia covers the team from the 1930s through the 1980s.

The Yanks have
graced more World
Series programs than
any other team.

Programs and guides from the '50s, including a Mickey Mantle "talking baseball card," which played Mantle's voice.

The Yankees were always coverboys. Here, Mickey and Casey grace two covers of *Life,* watched by a bobbing-head Yankee doll. Far right, a 1960 "jay" program (unofficial, with no ads).

Above, a Berra commemorative plate.

"Look at the talent on those teams," said Mickey Mantle recently, eyes wide at the memory. "We had a great pitching staff. When I came up in 1951 we had Whitey Ford, Eddie Lopat, Vic Raschi, and Allie Reynolds. Later on, we still had Whitey and we had Bob Turley and Ralph Terry. The lineup was powerful. We had Roger and I in the middle of the order and guys like Skowron, McDougald, Bauer, and Richardson. Yogi was the best catcher in baseball, and if he wasn't, then [Elston] Howard was."

And there was a union between the players and fans that was remarkable.

Lawrence Peter Berra, known to the world simply as "Yogi," was the originator, or mis-originator, of more famous lines than Henny Youngman and Benjamin Franklin combined.

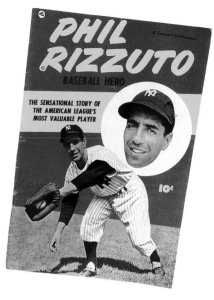

The Phil Rizzuto Story. Look at that form! Holy cow!

I've been a Yankee fan since age eleven. I lived in the same town as Phil Rizzuto then and I knew where he lived. Each morning, I'd pedal my bike over to his house and just sit there for hours 'till he came out, and then talked to him, clowned around, got autographs. He was wonderful. Everybody loved him. Later when I was a teenager, I lived near Newark and went to all the Newark Bears [then the Yanks' farm club] games. I found out where Bobby Brown, who later went to the Yankees, lived and I'd take the same bus home with him from the ballpark so I could talk to him. I did everything a kid could do to hang out with those guys. What a time. . . .

—SEYMOUR SPIEGEL, 57, of Watchung, New Jersey, who spends his yearly vacations watching Yankee spring training in Florida

"Today, 50 percent of every team is brand new. In the '50s, the Yankees were the same year after year," observed '50's Yankee shortstop Gil McDougald. "You could go to the ballpark any spring and see me or Rizzuto at short, Moose or Joe Collins at first, Richardson at second, Yogi behind the plate, Whitey on the mound, and the Mick in center. The Yankees were a family and we were a familiar family with our fans. Kids grew into young men watching the same Yankee team. There was a special bond there that didn't exist anywhere else."

McDougald was wrong about that last bit. There was another team with a similar bond to its fans, and it was just a few subway stops away in the great republic of Brooklyn. The Dodger faithful loved their team just as much, if not more, and it was the collision of these two great teams with their two great families of fans that made both franchises the stuff of legend.

The Yankees won pennants in eight years between 1947 and 1956, and in six of them they met the Dodgers in the historic Subway Series.

The drama started in the fourth game of the '47 Series when journeyman Yankee starter Floyd Bevens, who had finished the season with a lackluster 7–13 record, found himself in the ninth inning with a no-

The traditional Ballantine team photo, this one from 1954. Quick, make the three ring sign. . . .

A 1953 Yankees team button.

hitter. But with two men on, Dodger pinch-hitter Cookie Lavagetto rifled a double off the right-field wall, a hit that not only broke up the no-hitter but won the game. Bevens was crushed. The Yankees won game five, lost six on a great catch by Dodger left-fielder Al Gionfriddo, and won the seventh, 5–2.

Two years later, in 1949, the Yankees slipped into the Series by beating the Red Sox for the pennant on the last day of the season. Stumbling in the back door, they faced a powerful Dodger team led by Jackie Robinson, Roy Campanella, and big Don Newcombe, and although they won the Series four games to one, in only one outing was the margin more than two runs.

The Yanks won the Series again in 1950, this time against Philadelphia, but Brooklyn emerged as their greatest rival once more in 1951. The Dodgers had wrapped up the pennant by August 12 with an almost insurmountable 13½-game lead over the cross-town New York Giants. But the scrappy Giants, led by slugging rookie Willie Mays, slowly crept up on the Dodgers, forced them into a pennant playoff, and skipped into the World Series, where they were thrashed by the Yankees four games to two.

The 1952 Series again pitted the Dodgers against a Yankee team that was

**Yogi and Mickey
pushing Yoo Hoo.**

**Samples of old soda
bottle caps.**

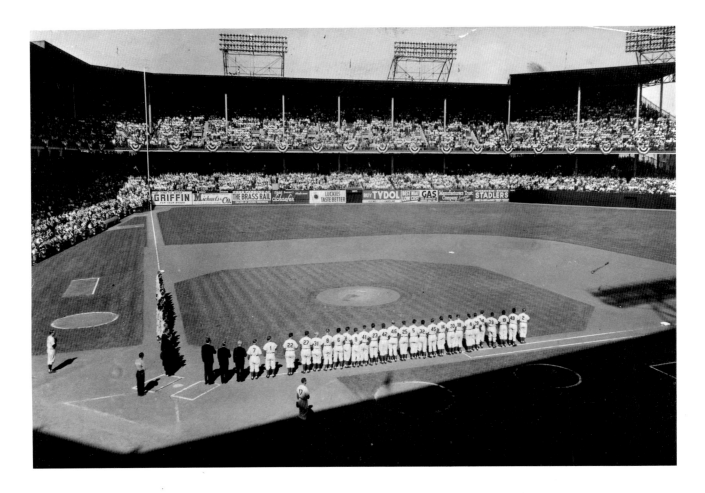

World Series glory: the Yankees and the Dodgers line up for pre-game ceremonies during the 1953 World Series at Brooklyn's Ebbets Field.

growing stronger year by year. This one was another thriller, with the Dodgers taking a quick lead, three games to one, and the Yankees fighting back to knot the Series three to three. In game seven, sheer luck and a plucky play by Billy "the Kid" Martin determined the Yanks' fate. The Bronx Bombers led 4–2 when reliever Bob Kuzava came in with the bases loaded

and one out in the seventh inning. Under Kuzava's pressure Duke Snider popped out for number two. Then Jackie Robinson stepped up and he too hit a pop fly that looked for all the world like the final out. But first baseman Joe Collins lost the ball in the sun, and no one else knew where it was either. Disaster seemed imminent when suddenly, from a dead stop at second

70

Right, Billy Martin, whose hit won the Yanks' fifth straight World Series in 1953, hugged by Phil Rizzuto on his right.

base, Martin charged toward home plate at top speed and made a sensational shoe-string catch as the ball kissed the top of the grass in front of home. Flipping the ball to the umpire like it was a routine play, Martin just kept on running into the dug-out, saving the inning, the game, and the Series.

In 1953 the Dodgers had an even stronger team with five .300 hitters in the lineup. Led by the slugging of Roy Campa-nella, the club was so powerful that it won the pennant thirteen games ahead of the Braves. Sportswriters were certain the Dodgers would finally beat the Yankees in the Series. But the Bronx Bombers won another one, four games to two, driving Brooklyn fans to despair.

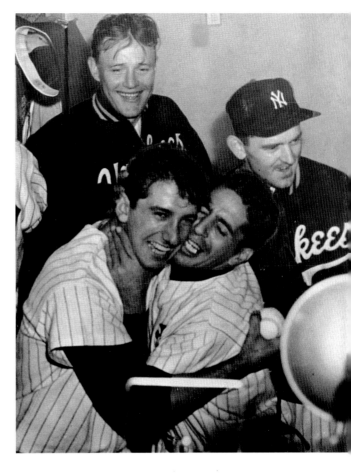

A 1954 Yanks program.

Neither the Dodgers nor the Yan-kees could win the pennant in 1954. In a stunning surprise, the Cleveland Indians won a record 111 games that season to beat out the Yanks for the pennant while the Giants triumphed over the Dodgers.

The next year it was back to business as usual for the Yanks and Dodgers as the two clubs clashed again in October. Led by

71

Series moved down the subway tracks to Brooklyn, the Dodgers took three straight. Back at Yankee Stadium steady pitching by Ford claimed game six for the Yanks, but in game seven it was all Brooklyn. Johnny Podres pitched shutout ball and in the sixth inning Sandy Amoros made one of the great catches of all time in left field to rob Yogi Berra of a triple that would have driven in two runs. Brooklyn had beaten the "damn Yankees" at last.

The final Yankee-Dodger World Series was in 1956, and appropriately it was in this last clash before the Dodgers

Gwen Verdon graced the cover of a 1955 *Time* magazine in *Damn Yankees,* a musical about how the Devil broke up the Yankee dynasty. Everyone else sure couldn't.

New York newspapers printed season schedules like this one from 1955 in their Sunday centerfolds. The open schedule fit nicely on a kid's closet door.

Mantle and Berra and the pitching of Ford (18–7), Bob Turley (17–13), and Tommy Byrne (16–5), the Bronx Bombers were good. But the Dodgers were great. The Bums from Brooklyn won their first ten games that season, took twenty-two of their first twenty-four, and won the flag by 13½ games despite a late-season slump. They charged into October smelling a world championship at last.

It seemed like old times as the Yanks won the first two games, but when the

72

A sample packet of team player photos popular with fans in the '50s. Today, a single packet can cost up to $200.

fled to the West Coast that the most memorable moment of all occurred. Journeyman Yankee pitcher Don Larsen, who had posted a thoroughly unimpressive 11–5 record during the regular season, was shelled in the second inning of the second game, but to the disappointment of many fans he returned to start game five, with the Series tied two up. The game was played on October 8 at Yankee Stadium, where there were 67,000 seats for the fifty-six million who now swear they were there.

Larsen, striking out few and throwing incidental fastballs, moved along inning by inning until by the end of the eighth he and everyone else knew that he was at legend's doorstep. He was three outs away

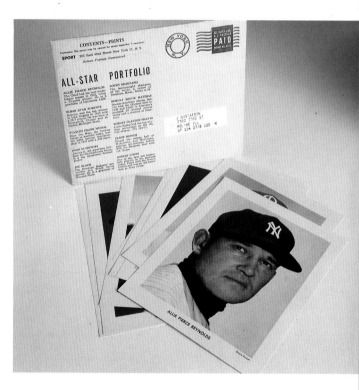

Star-studded Yankee lighter from the '50s.

from the first and only perfect game in World Series history.

Yogi Berra still argues that Larsen would never have done it if the score had not been so close, 2–0. "If it was 9–0 he would have been paying little attention," Berra insists. "It was close and he had to be extremely disciplined. He was. At the start of the ninth I didn't say a thing about how well he was throwing. I went to the mound and reminded him that if he walked one guy and the next guy hit one out the game was tied."

73

LARSEN'S PERFECT GAME

You're never supposed to talk about a no-hitter to the pitcher, but I didn't even realize he had one going. When we went out for the eighth, I saw the scoreboard with all those zeros and I just blurted out to him, "Hey, Don, you've got a no-hitter going!" He laughed and blushed and I think maybe that broke the tension for him, it being that sudden and all.

—MICKEY MANTLE, New York Yankees

The third strike on Dale Mitchell was absolutely, positively a strike on the outside corner. No question about it. People say it was a ball and that I rushed the mound to hug Larsen to make the ump think it was a strike. Nonsense. It was a perfect strike.

—YOGI BERRA, New York Yankees

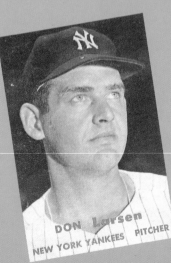

Don Larsen's 1957 baseball card.

The scoreboard behind Don Larsen tells the story as he throws the final pitch of his perfect game in the 1956 World Series.

The Yankees sold these "Perfect Game" commemorative plates for $3 in 1956.

The Perfect Game

WORLD SERIES 5TH GAME

OCTOBER 8TH 1956

Perfection - Start to Finish

Dodgers—000 000 000–0
Yankees—000 101 00x–2

I f we were ahead eight or nine to nothing, he would never have had the perfect game. People forget the score was just 2–0. At the start of the last inning, I told him, "Hey, one guy gets on and the next guy hits one out and we're tied." That's all I could think about and that's all he could think about. He was very careful and disciplined with his pitches because the game could still be lost.

—YOGI BERRA, New York Yankees

The scoreboard shows:

	1	2	3	4	5	6	7	8	9	10	R	H	E
KLYN.	0	0	0	0	0	0	0				0	0	0
NKS	0	0	1	0	1	0	0				2	5	0

AT BAT 8 POS. BALL 1 STRIKE 2 OUT 2

Don Larsen as he throws the final pitch of his perfect game in the 1956 World Series.

Larsen didn't walk anyone. He got final batter Dale Mitchell on a called third strike on the corner and bedlam broke loose in the stadium as Berra rushed the mound and jumped into Larsen's arms. Amid the tumult one fan stole Larsen's cap.

Although the Dodgers only won one of the Series, they remember them as fondly as the Yankees. Duke Snider, who played center field for the Dodgers in those years, still thinks they rank among the greatest of sporting events.

"You had two very fine ball clubs which got into the Series by beating very fine clubs like the Indians and the Giants and the Red Sox. You had great players on those teams in those years. Look at those lineups. Robinson, Pee Wee Reese, Carl

This trio of baseballs is signed by Willie, Mickey, and the Duke. So who *was* the best center fielder?

My most vivid memory of going to see the Yankees in the '50s and '60s was riding the subway up to the stadium. The cars were packed with people and absolutely everybody was going to the game. You'd talk about the game to total strangers on the train like they were your brothers. Then, when the train pulled into the stadium stop the entire subway would unload and this river of people would charge down the subway platform towards the stadium as the train pulled out—totally empty.

—FRANK RUBANO, 48, of Carbondale, Pennsylvania

Furillo, Johnny Podres, Gil Hodges, Roy Campanella, Mantle, Ford, Berra, Bauer, Collins, McDougald. You had the city rivalry, the Subway Series.

"The most important thing though," continues Snider, "the thing that made them so wonderful, was that a team would bring thousands of its fans across town to the other team's ballpark. In most Series, your away game is in enemy territory. Here, you had your fans with you all the time. It was great for the players and the fans. Those series really made New York fans feel a part of baseball forever."

AFTER CASEY
1960–1973

The Yankee juggernaut continued to roll throughout the 1950s. The men in pinstripes took the pennant again in 1957 and 1958, but lost to the Milwaukee Braves in the '57 World Series. The White Sox somehow sneaked in and took the flag in '59, but the Yanks bounced back to win in 1960. The same horses that carried them through the heady early years of the decade helped them gallop through the last.

In addition to Mantle, the Yanks had solid hitting during these years from Yogi Berra, Elston Howard, Gil McDougald, Moose Skowron, Tony Kubek, Hank Bauer, Andy Carey, Bobby Richardson, and Joe Collins. And the team had superb pitching from Ralph Terry, Bob Turley, Ford, Johnny Kucks, Don Larsen, Art Ditmar, and Bobby Shantz.

Ford was the "money" pitcher on the team, the man who won the big ones and a pinpoint pitcher who could mix up his pitches to fool anyone. When he came up as a rookie in 1951 he immediately registered a 9–1 record. His ERAs were always low, (in eleven of sixteen seasons below 3.00), the sign of a man who controlled the game. Ford pitched forty-five shutouts and won eight 1–0 games. Stengel protected him, using him sparingly, but when Ralph Houk became manager he put Ford in his four-day rotations and Whitey promptly won twenty-five games. He has the highest single-season winning percentage of any pitcher with twenty wins.

Mickey Mantle as a rookie in 1951. Even today, people who shake hands with Mantle are in awe of the size and strength of his hands and fore-arms, the sources of his amazing power. The Mick hit .300 in ten seasons, smashed 536 home runs, and hit eighteen round trippers in World Series play, a record.

A baseball sketch set starring **Yogi Berra**, left center.

Opposite, **Whitey Ford** memorabilia featuring every Whitey collectible you could think of.

I had an arrangement with the Yankees to cut the season short so I could go back to medical school and become a doctor. I had an arrangement with the medical school to study while playing with the Yankees. Every night I read *Gray's Anatomy,* the big, thick medical encyclopedia. Night after night, Yogi kept asking me how it was going and I kept saying fine, and kept reading. Finally, at the end of the season, I slammed the back cover shut. I was finished.

"So, Bobby," Yogi said to me, "did the book have a happy ending?"

—BOBBY BROWN, New York Yankees

"Great pitcher?" Ford laughs. "Me? Hell, my wife'd be a great pitcher with those guys in the lineup getting her runs!"

A little exaggeration, maybe, but Ford did have great battery mates in Yogi Berra and Elston Howard. Berra was the odd man in the lineup—he would have been in any lineup. A short, stocky, barrel-shaped man with a wide face and large ears, he looked more like a circus figure than a Hall-of-Famer. But the man sure could hit. Yogi had 306 homers lifetime to go with five 100-RBI seasons. He was a good bad-ball hitter, picking up dozens of hits on low outside pitches, which he would golf into the outfield, and high fast-balls, which he would chop down the line. He was a terrific clutch hitter who rarely struck out. And his wit was legendary: "You can see a lot by observing"—"A nickel ain't worth a dime anymore"—"Nobody goes to that restaurant anymore, it's too crowded."

Ford was also supported by the long-underpraised Elston Howard, one of the best catchers of his day and a man always overshadowed by Yogi. He played outfield his first five years in deference to Yogi, but when he moved behind the plate he was impressive. Howard made the All-Star team nine times, had three .300-plus seasons, hit .348 in 1961, and was named the league MVP in 1963. When he was finally

traded to Boston in 1967, he promptly helped the Sox take the pennant too.

Moose Skowron, a burly first baseman with a remarkable, rugged face, became a mainstay of the Yankee infield during much of the '50s. He came up in '54 to replace Joe Collins and then hit .300 in five different seasons. He got key hits, late-inning hits, and many extra base hits with his powerful swing.

Despite their solid performance during the '50s, the decade ended on a sour

More than just one of the great Yankee pitchers, Whitey Ford has the highest winning percentage of any twentieth-century pitcher (.694) with his 236–106 record.

Right, a signed ball along with Whitey's Babe Ruth Award, given to the outstanding player of the 1961 World Series.

In my whole career, I never looked up once at a home run. You don't want to embarrass the pitcher. But on the ball I nearly hit over the roof at Yankee Stadium, I just had to look up. Jack Fisher was pitching and he threw me a perfect, hard fastball, right over the middle of the plate. I swung as hard as I've ever swung and as soon as it left the bat I knew it was fair and I also knew it was the longest ball I'd ever hit. So I looked up to see how far it would go. It kept going up and I thought it would go over the roof, but it hit the facade about two feet from the top and bounced back. When it hit, I put my head down and continued my trot. I never hit a ball that hard again.

—MICKEY MANTLE, New York Yankees

One of our guys was the victim of a knock-down pitch the previous inning, so the first batter knew I'd knock him down. It was Mickey. I thought I'd fool him and lay one right over, knowing he'd be getting ready to hit the dirt. Well, he forgot about the knock down and was just standing there. It was a perfect fastball. It was the longest home run ever hit off me.

—PEDRO RAMOS, Washington Senators

367 Feet

108 Ft. 1 In.

Mickey Mantle made baseball history when he missed by only six inches hitting the first fair ball out of Yankee Stadium.

Dotted lines indicate the path of the ball during the Yankee–Kansas City game, May 22, 1956.

These exhibit cards of Whitey Ford, Elston Howard, and Yogi Berra were popular in the early '60s.

Bill "Moose" Skowron, longtime Yankee first baseman.

I never had a lucky glove or a lucky uniform. A glove was nothing more than a glove to me. They bronzed the glove I wore the day I broke Babe Ruth's scoreless inning World Series record, but I still don't know why. People think there's something special about the glove a pitcher wears, but I don't. The glove I had on that day was just another glove, that's all. The glove doesn't throw the ball. The glove means nothing to me. Still doesn't.

—WHITEY FORD, New York Yankees

The Yankees did not win the World Series every year—it just seemed that way. In one of the most dramatic finishes to any sporting event, the Pittsburgh Pirates' Bill Mazeroski hit a tenth inning home run off Yank hurler Ralph Terry to win the '60 Series.

note for the Bronx Bombers. After the White Sox took the American League flag in 1959, the Yanks lost the '60 Series to the Pittsburgh Pirates on a tenth-inning seventh-game home run by Bill Mazeroski off a dejected Ralph Terry. And then months later the Yanks fired the Ol' Perfessor, Casey Stengel, claiming that at 70 he was just too old to manage anymore. Players, fans, and other baseball execs were stunned. Casey had been one of the most successful managers of all time, certainly one of the most popular, and for his efforts at bringing the Yankees so much glory he had been canned.

Pitcher Ralph Terry, who bounced back from losing the '60 World Series to become MVP of the '61 Series.

A 1960 World Series ticket for the bleachers—$2.10.

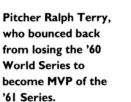

85

MICKEY MANTLE

An inventive 1962 entrepreneur sold All-Star stationery, here picturing Mantle.

Why did I fall in love with the Yankees? Two words, baby—Mickey Mantle.

—CHRIS KIRCH, 38

Mickey Mantle's Isometric Minute-a-Day Gym ("Invest 1 minute a day and have the muscles and physique of an athlete, without strain, without sweat, without exhaustive exercises"), accompanied by other Mantle-obilia.

Right, this collage celebrates Mickey's great achievements.

Following a New
York ritual, brave
fans camp out at
Yankee Stadium the
night before tickets
go on sale in 1961.

Ralph Houk, "the Major" (he had been a major in the U.S. Army in World War II), replaced Casey at the helm. Supplied with sluggers and great pitchers, Houk did little more than turn on the ignition key each day and let the car drive itself. The Yanks under Houk won world championships in 1961 and 1962, and a pennant in 1963. But the likable Houk was kicked upstairs by Yankee management after the Dodgers won the '63 Series in a four-game sweep. He returned to the dugout from 1966 to 1973 as the team's manager and then moved on to manage the Tigers and the Red Sox, finishing his career with a very respectable .514 won-lost percentage.

It was during Houk's first year as manager that the Home Run Derby between Mickey Mantle, Roger Maris, and the ghost of Babe Ruth took place. For an entire season, Mantle and Maris battled each other and Ruth's legacy for the most cherished hitting record in baseball, sixty home runs in a single season. The race cre-

88

ated a carnival atmosphere in Yankee Stadium and in any ballpark they visited. Mantle and Maris were the home-run twins and for that single magical summer, the greatest show on earth.

Years before, in a letter now owned by collector Barry Halper, Babe Ruth had predicted that the man to break his home-run record would be a power hitter batting in the number three spot followed by a power hitter batting in the number four spot. And that's exactly what happened. No pitcher could risk throwing around Maris because Mantle was up next. The two pulverized pitchers. They devoured fastballs, curve balls, and changeups, demolishing lefties and righties with equal disdain.

When Mantle was injured late in the season, his production slowed, but Maris plunged on toward history. Number sixty-one came on the final day of the season—

Y ou know one reason I love the Yankees? Because the Yankees stayed in New York where they were loved. The Giants and Dodgers betrayed all New Yorkers when they fled to the West Coast. The Yankees stayed with their people and I love 'em for that.

—JOHN CLEARY, 36

These days, Mantle spends much of his time autographing fan items like this bat and picture.

A signed Mantle-Ford print celebrating the two great Hall-of-Famers.

Mantle and Maris in the splendid summer of 1961, when they combined for a record 115 home runs.

at Yankee Stadium against the Red Sox. The joy was muted, however, because Commissioner Ford Frick ruled that since Roger hit sixty-one in a 162-game season —Ruth's were in a 154-game schedule— the record would carry an asterisk (which was dropped in 1991). The sportswriters and fans never took a liking to Maris either, and the jubilation that should have been there wasn't.

"And that's a shame," says Mantle today. "People just never got to know him well enough. He was a great player and a good and decent man."

Mantle and Maris pins.

Roger Maris hits his record-breaking sixty-first home run in the very last game of the 1961 season.

The 1961 Yankees, said to be as good as the 1927 Yankees, which many consider the greatest team ever to play the game.

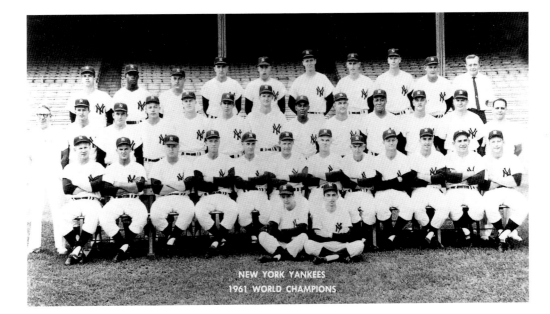

NEW YORK YANKEES
1961 WORLD CHAMPIONS

T he first time I saw the Yankees it was the early '60s, maybe '61. I was a kid and the Yankees beat up on whomever they were playing that day. They hit seven home runs. Seven! They scored something like fifteen runs! They didn't let up. Not once. I hated them because they were so good. Nobody on this earth should be that good at anything, especially baseball. I have hated them ever since. I never admired Mickey Mantle. I hated Mickey Mantle. These last few years, when the Yankees have been struggling, have been the happiest years of my life.

—BILL CLARK, 38

A Mickey Mantle glove in its Mickey Mantle box, accompanied by a Mantle Zippo lighter.

91

ROGER MARIS

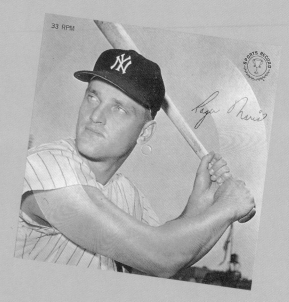

People just remember the sixty-one home runs. They forget that Roger was an excellent base stealer and a superb right fielder. He was the best defensive right fielder in the majors. He was an all-around ballplayer, a humble guy, a real team player. History never gave him his due.

—BILL "MOOSE" SKOWRON,
New York Yankees

Above right, Maris "talking baseball card," a 33 RPM record that doubled as a card. Below, Maris as cover boy.

It's a disgrace that Roger Maris isn't in the Hall of Fame. He was the most underrated baseball player of all time. Everybody said all he ever did was hit sixty-one home runs. Well, who else hit sixty-one home runs? People forget that the year before, he hit thirty-nine. That's a hundred in two years. Only Ruth hit a hundred in two successive years. Roger was the American League MVP two years in a row. . . . Roger was also a vastly underrated base runner. He was fast and he was smart. He was a genius at breaking up double plays with his slides into second. He was a canny and effective right fielder. I can't remember a ball ever getting by Roger or Roger making a bad throw. He was the complete ball-player and for a few years as powerful a slugger as Ruth.

—RALPH TERRY, New York Yankees

One fan in New York collects everything ever produced on Maris, including a Maris wiffle ball, in the middle.

A Roger Maris baseball board game.

My father loved Roger Maris. My most vivid memory of childhood was watching a Yankee game late in the '61 season, when Maris was pulling close to Ruth's record sixty homers. Dad and I watched the game on a TV in my room. My mother came in and yelled at him for keeping me up so late, so he told me to go to sleep, turned off the sound, and watched the picture by himself. About an hour later, me in deep sleep, he shakes me and scares me to death. "Get up! Get up! Maris just hit fifty-eight."

—Broadcaster HOWIE ROSE, WFAN

Mickey in 1966 after yet more surgery on his fragile left knee. Even though he played with injuries all of his career (he first tore his knee as a rookie), Mantle is very proud of the fact that he played more games than any other Yankee, including Lou Gehrig.

A four-foot-high Mantle bean-bag game from Frank Palmer's collection: the irony is that you get the most points for whacking the Mick's bad knee.

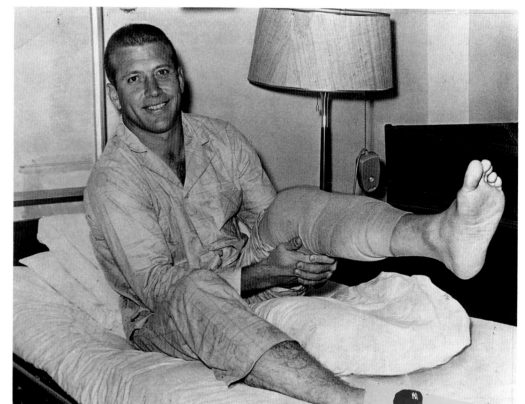

grew up in Detroit and my dad was a Tiger fan. He took me to my first game when I was, oh, eleven or twelve. It was against the Yankees, with Mickey Mantle and Roger Maris. I fell head over heels in love with the Yankees that day. I don't know what it was. I don't even remember if the Mick or Maris hit a home run, but they were my team on the spot—and ever since.

—GABE POMPE, 35

The Yanks were big on medallions and pins, including this World Series pin and a '67 Mother's Day pin.

The Bronx Bombers roared into the World Series that year and beat the Cincinnati Reds easily, four games to one. The team went on to win pennants in 1962, 1963, and 1964, and claimed the World Series again in 1962. But even as the players took their bows in the field, an era was ending.

Although the Yankees won the pennant in 1964 with Yogi Berra as manager, there was considerable dissension on the team. Players suggested that while Yogi was a wonderful person, he was a lackluster manager. The next year Yogi was gone, and Johnny Keane, the manager of the very same Cardinals who beat the Yankees in the 1964 World Series, was hired to pilot the team. But the fans didn't like him and neither did the players. They said he was too old, not a New York manager, and too distant from the players. The team slipped to sixth place, the lowest it had

been since late 1925. At the same time that managerial problems were setting in, the on-field staff began to collapse due to aging and injuries. And then in 1966 the unthinkable happened—the mighty Bronx Bombers finished dead last.

The team stumbled through the rest of the '60s, finishing no better than fourth. Fans and sportswriters leveled the blame at everyone: at CBS, the team's new owners, for not beefing up the minor leagues; at new president Mike Burke for not being a baseball man; at the scouts for not finding talent; at the veteran players for being too old and the young players for not being old enough. Nothing worked. An empire had fallen.

A pair of eyeglasses worn by fastballer Ryne Duren, noted for his glasses and his lack of control.

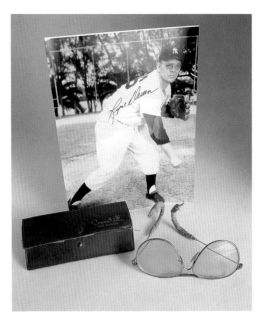

STEINBRENNER AND THE MODERN AGE
1973–1978

On June 3, 1973, CBS sold the New York Yankees to an investment group headed by George Steinbrenner, who owned a Cleveland ship-building company. New Yorkers knew nothing about him, but they would soon know too much. Steinbrenner would become the most controversial owner in baseball history, a face that appeared in the papers so often that he would be as recognizable on the streets of New York as a movie star. Sportswriters and fans would denounce him on radio shows and in newspaper interviews because they felt, and still feel, that he meddled too much in the running of the club. Baseball experts would complain bitterly about his constant hiring and firing of Billy Martin as manager. Players would scorn him, vendors would howl about him, and lawyers would mutter under their breath about him.

None of this ever bothered George. His goal was to win. He bought a loser and he intended to make it a winner, and to do it, he opened up a wallet that would make Donald Trump cringe. The year he arrived, 1973, was the beginning of free agency in baseball, which allowed players whose contracts had expired to sign with whomever they wanted. They all wanted to sign with Steinbrenner.

He wanted the best pitcher in baseball, so he paid $3.35 million for Jim "Catfish" Hunter. He wanted the top slugger, so he paid $2.66 million

"The straw that stirs the drink"—Yankee extraordinaire Reggie Jackson.

Controversial Yankee owner George Steinbrenner wanted his team to be the best in baseball, and by the late '70s, after the infusion of much cash, his wish had been granted.

for Reggie Jackson. He also got pitcher Don Gullett ($2.09 million) and Rich "Goose" Gossage, the game's top reliever ($2.75 million). He dismissed team president Larry MacPhail, fired Ralph Houk as manager, and sold or traded half the team, bringing in stars like Graig Nettles, Lou Piniella, and Chris Chambliss. Caricatured by cartoonist Bill Gallo as a figure called General Von Steingrabber, he intended to win the pennant, no matter what the cost.

And Steinbrenner, quickly nicknamed "the Boss" by the New York press, did

just that. His brand-new Yankee team stumbled for a few seasons, then took its first pennant in 1976. Two more followed in 1977 and 1978 along with two world championships. The Yankees were back, and in style.

"I had mixed feelings about coming to the Yankees because all that fame and glory was in the past," admitted Willie Randolph, who came from the Pittsburgh Pirates and would go on to play in the Bronx for a decade, becoming team captain. "When I arrived at Yankee Stadium

a decade," he continued. "The old glory was meaningless. We won the Series in 1977 and in April 1978 I remember one night I was on the field and I found myself staring down at the pinstripes on my uniform. It was then and only then that I felt the glory and tradition that was the Yankees. We were champions, too, this '70s team, and we finally belonged to that glory and tradition. I got goose bumps. Ruth and Gehrig and all of that legendary stuff just swept over me that night out there on the field. I was a Yankee at last."

Above, Willie Randolph, a Yankee captain in the '70s.

Right, one of the best pitchers of the '70s, Jim "Catfish" Hunter.

I'd look at all those trophies and pictures of Ruth and Gehrig and DiMaggio and hear all these stories about pennants and World Series but, honestly, it meant nothing to me. Hey, I was a Mets fan.

"We were a different Yankee team, the '70s team, and we hadn't done much in

For you...from

REGGIE!

SPECIAL MAIL-IN OFFER
REGGIE JACKSON
AUTOGRAPHED TO YOU
BASEBALL
AND TROPHY CASE
Only $3.50

36
COUNT

TAKE ONE

REGGIE!

Chocolaty covered caramel and peanuts

Jackson always said he wanted his own candy bar and he finally got one, the "Reggie." But when he struck out fans would throw the candy at him.

was a teenager in the late '70s and I liked the Yankees. Then in '77 and '78 they had those two world champion teams and I fell in love with them. It wasn't just the idea of being the best—it was the guys. Reggie hitting those three home runs in that one last Series game. A scriptwriter for a movie couldn't write that ending. Or Guidry winning twenty-five, or Bucky Dent winning the playoff game with that home run over the wall in Boston. They were so . . . so . . . dramatic. God, they were great.

—Broadcaster STEVE MARLZBURG

The Yankee teams of that era were powerhouses with fine talent, just like the teams of the '50s and '20s. The 1977 team assembled by Steinbrenner had three men who hit over .300 (Thurman Munson, Mickey Rivers, and Lou Piniella). Graig Nettles hit thirty-seven home runs and 107 RBIs, and Reggie Jackson smashed thirty-two homers and 110 RBIs. Ron Guidry was 16–7 and an incredible 25–3 in 1978. That year Ed Figueroa went 20–9, Sparky Lyle was the top reliever in baseball, Thurman Munson was the best catcher (yes, including Johnny Bench) and Reggie—well, Reggie was Reggie.

Even Steinbrenner seemed humble compared to Reggie. No sooner had Jackson arrived in the Big Apple than he announced that he, not Munson, would be the team's leader, declaring, "I'm the straw that stirs the drink." He fought with Billy Martin for years, argued with sportswriters, and even had a candy bar named after him. Most of all, Reggie produced. Already a star in Oakland, in his first four years in New York he hit 129 home runs, drove in 407 RBIs, and batted .291, leading the Yankees to consecutive world championships. He snared a piece of immortality on the way, hitting three consecutive home runs in game six of the '77 Series, all on the first pitch.

A bat company in Cooperstown, New York, makes team bats like this Yankee model, and fans try to get players to sign it. Next to it is a signed Reggie Jackson bat.

I knew something great was going to happen that day, I just knew it. I felt good all day, real loose, real "up." In batting practice I must have hit twelve home runs, and they were all long ones. The crowd was cheering wildly for me in batting practice. [In the game] I got up, on the first homer, and, Jesus, I could feel it in my bat. I was hot all over. The first pitch was right in there, just exactly where I like it. I swung. Bang! Gone. I knew I was going to do that, I just knew it. Next time up, I could feel it again. First pitch. Bang! Gone! Number two. Then I got up again and the crowd was really roaring. They were stomping their feet and 60,000 of them were chanting my name, REGGIE! REGGIE! REGGIE! God, was I pumped up. It was a different pitcher now, and I didn't know what to expect. First pitch—right down the middle. I swung and hit it out. I felt like Superman. I'm telling you, if they had tied it up and we played eight more extra innings, I'd have hit three more home runs on the first pitch that night.

—REGGIE JACKSON, New York Yankees

A signed Reggie Jackson poster.

101

YANKEE STADIUM

I loved to steal bases when I was a kid and played in Little League. I never got caught, not once. After I slid in, I'd stand up and close my eyes real tight and pretend I was in Yankee Stadium and the crowd was roaring for me. Then I'd open my eyes and look around and I could see the Stadium all around me at the Little League field. I was in the World Series, and all that red, white, and blue bunting was draped over the rails and the place was packed and I'd look up and see that big [blue-painted] copper facade and the sky above it. All I wanted to do was grow up and play in Yankee Stadium.

—JOHNNY BENCH, Cincinnati Reds

The exterior of the House That Stein-brenner Remodeled. The $100 million renovation of the stadium in 1973 resulted in fewer seats and no overhanging facades as well as a handsome exterior and a sensational, brightly lit sign.

Opposite, Reggie sliding with typical flair.

YANKEE STADIUM

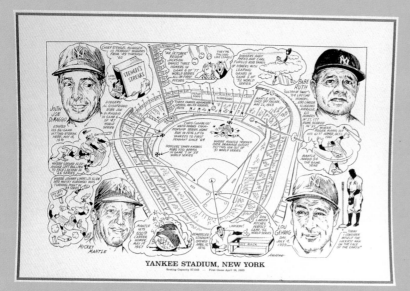

YANKEE STADIUM, NEW YORK
Seating Capacity 67,345 · First Game April 18, 1923

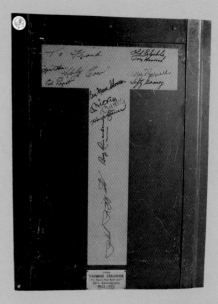

Above, the Yankee Stadium illustration from a popular stadium series.

Upper right, this letter *T*, signed by nearly a dozen Yankee greats, came from the old Stadium scoreboard.

Below, this plaque commemorating the greatest Yankees was mounted on the Stadium Club wall for years.

Yankee Stadium people just loved good baseball. In 1946 right after the season we were on an All-Star team that barnstormed with a Negro League All-Star team. We booked Yankee Stadium not thinking we'd draw much of a crowd—we played the same day as a World Series game in Saint Louis. We pulled 47,000 people to that game in the Stadium, more than the World Series drew.

—BOB FELLER, Cleveland Indians

Old Yankee Stadium diagram folders, which you could check after you'd bought your ticket to see if you were stuck behind a pillar.

If Yankee Stadium wasn't as big, who knows how many home runs I'd hit there. One day in the early '80s I walked around out there to look at the fences now, which are much closer than when I played. Right about where the fence was built is where a lot of balls I hit would come down. I think if I played there today, with the shorter center area fences, I'd hit, oh, ten to twelve more homers a year than I did.

—MICKEY MANTLE, New York Yankees

Left, this painting was the centerfold image from a 1936 issue of *Esquire,* signed by then-rookie DiMaggio. Although Ruth had left the team in '35, Number 3 is still shown in the on-deck circle.

Below, the rules and regulations of the Stadium Club were spelled out on this plaque, which was removed from the old stadium when it was renovated.

The stadium is death to right-handed power hitters now, and it was worse before the 1973 renovations. Center field used to be 467 feet deep and left and right center were almost as deep. Balls that would be home runs anywhere on the planet were just long outs. Home run hitters died in center field there.

—BUD HARRELSON, erstwhile manager of the New York Mets who played in Yankee Stadium as a young Met

Thurman Munson's cap and signed ball.

Above, a Munson autographed bat, and, below, a memorial button.

Reggie may have been the media star, but the team's rugged, brusk, hard-nosed catcher, Thurman Munson, was its backbone. Munson came up to the big leagues after only 100 games in the minor leagues and became a star right away for manager Ralph Houk, hitting .302 and winning American League rookie-of-the-year honors. He got better and better. He hit over .300 in 1976, 1977, and 1978, leading the Yankees to three straight pennants. The front office thought so much of him he was named captain, but there was no bright future for Munson, who died in a tragic plane crash on August 2, 1979.

The year before Munson's death, 1978, was a hot year for a number of Yan-

**Above, pitcher Ron
Guidry, AKA Louisi-
ana Lightnin'.**

kees, and none more than pitcher Ron
"Louisiana Lightnin' " Guidry. He not only
won twenty-five games but his three losses
were all by only a few runs; with some
luck, he could have been 28–0. Looking
back, he now believes that a lot of the success he had came from not thinking about
what he was doing.

"In the first half of the season, no
pitcher pays any attention to his record.
You could win six and lose the next six
just as easily. That happens all the time.
Towards the end of the year, my only concern, everybody's only concern, was somehow catching the Red Sox. I paid so much
attention to that that my own wins didn't
mean much. I can honestly say that I didn't

**Guidry on a program
cover from '83.**

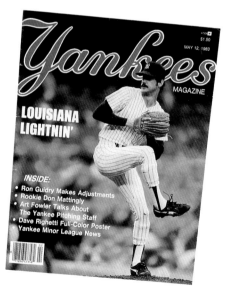

Tommy John's and Thurman Munson's jerseys.

A Yankee promotional penknife from 1978.

know, and still don't know, when I won game twenty, or twenty-five. If I had to think about it, I doubt I would have pitched so well."

Guidry, like Jackson and everybody else, thinks the '77 and '78 Yanks were among the best clubs ever. "We had pitching with Ed [Figueroa], Sparky [Lyle], Gullett, Mike Torrez, and Dick Tidrow. We had real power and speed in the lineup. Munson was a superstar. We had a very well balanced team. No weaknesses," he declared. "In '77 and '78, though, we had our hands full with the Red Sox."

Ah, the Red Sox. The Yankees–Red Sox rivalry had been dormant for years. The Red Sox hadn't needed the Yankees to ruin their dreams in the '60s and '70s, they had taken care of that by themselves. There had been bright spots, of course. In 1967 the miracle Sox moved from last to first but then, as usual, lost the World Series in seven games. They took the pennant again in '75 and again, as always, lost the World Series. These were the years when the Yankees were wandering through the deserts of the American League. In 1976, however, the Yankees returned to the top. The Bosox finished third in both 1976 and 1977, both pennant years for the Yanks, but in 1978 they threatened to run away with the American League.

WORLD
Yankees
CHAMPS
SPA-1

Sports Photo Assoc., Hawthorne, N.J. ©1979

The Red Sox were 14½ games ahead of the Yankees in mid-July. Billy Martin had been fired, again, and quiet Bob Lemon had taken over the dugout. The Bronx Bombers surged . . . unnoticed. They pulled closer and closer to the Red Sox. But even as they were winning forty-eight of sixty-eight, the Sox were folding. By September 4 the Yanks were just four back and pulled even by sweeping the Sox in Boston. The two archrivals finished the regular season tied and the first playoff since the Dodger-Giant battle of 1951 was ordered—one single game, do or die.

Boston jumped in front early, 2–0, and completely dominated the Yankees. After all those years, the Boston fans could finally sense victory over the hated Yan-kees. Then from out of nowhere a powder puff .143 hitter named Bucky Dent crashed a three-run home run over the Green Monster in the seventh inning, sealing the win for the Yankees. The moment couldn't have been sweeter.

**Bucky Dent crosses
the plate after hit-
ting the Fenway Park
home run that won
the one-game playoff
against Boston in '78.
Years later, Dent
was fired as manager
of the Yankees . . . in
Fenway Park.**

TOMORROW'S TEAM
1980s and On

The Yankees remained on top for several years, taking the divisional title in 1980 and the pennant in the strike-shortened 1981 season. They were beaten in the World Series by the Dodgers, though, an event that prompted Steinbrenner's embarrassing press conference at which he "apologized" to New York for the dismal Series performance.

The Yanks sagged to fifth in 1982 despite shelling out more money for more stars (Ken Griffey and Dave Collins) and then stumbled through the '80s. They had some good teams, finishing second several times and third twice, but they were never very close to first, and as the '90s began they slumped badly.

Fans were disappointed with the finishes but they certainly weren't disappointed with the players. Good fans know talent when they see it and the Yankee teams of the '80s were loaded with talent.

A multiple-player trade in 1985 engineered by Billy Martin brought in the mercurial Rickey Henderson, the all-time base-stealing and snatch-catch champ. He joined a lineup that included sluggers Dave Winfield and Don Mattingly. Henderson became a star immediately, the first American Leaguer to hit twenty home runs and steal fifty bases in a single season. That year he was third in the MVP voting and his 146 runs were the most

Yankee slugger Don Mattingly, team captain and guiding light. His .300-plus batting average and home run swing have carried the Yankees through the recent lean years and out into the dawn.

scored in the majors in nearly forty years. Rickey was also a speed demon, dancing off the bases and causing an excitement unknown on New York base paths since the days of Jackie Robinson. Unfortunately he was traded back to the Oakland A's in 1989 by a disappointed Yankee management, where of course he became a star all over again.

Teammate Dave Winfield was another player whom Steinbrenner courted and wrapped in money. Like Henderson, Winfield produced. He signed a ten-year contract in 1980 and starred right away, hitting .294 in 1981 and leading the Yanks to the World Series. Throughout his decade with the Bronx Bombers, Winfield was impressive, posting five straight 100-

Want to measure Tommy John's career? From his first start to his last, seven different presidents occupied the Oval Office. Hurling 26 years for different major league teams,

John came to the Yanks in 1979 and posted back-to-back 20 win seasons. The most amazing thing about his career, however, was his comeback from an arm injury in 1974.

From the '76 season, he pitched with a "bionic" arm that had been totally reconstructed by a team of doctors. His 288 wins fell just short of the 300 club.

A Dave Winfield fotoball.

Right, a watch commemorating Dave Righetti's 1983 no-hitter.

Below, Roy White graces this Nedicks giveaway cup.

RBI seasons, hitting twenty-four home runs in each of his seven full seasons with the team, and making the All-Star team twelve straight years. He had an uneasy relationship with Steinbrenner, however, and when his contract ran out he asked to be traded, moving to the California Angels and immediately starring there as well. They were joined by ace pitcher Tommy John, an imported star from L.A.

Winfield and Henderson were powerful and dramatic players, but no one's career during these years was more fascinating to watch than manager Billy Martin. His hirings and firings became a standard joke in New York, and at one point he and Steinbrenner even did a beer commercial with the firing as a punch line. Billy, a brash young player with the Bombers in the early '50s, had been a successful manager before moving to the Bronx in 1975 and

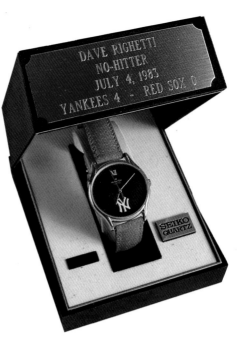

Even when the Yankees are in a down time, like the late '60s, the early '80s, now, they are always competitive. They play to win and they hate to lose. Look at Mattingly. That guy hates to lose. Look at Sax. The guy pops up and he throws his bat in disgust. You have to love a team that hates to lose, even when it does.

—TONY CANGIANO, 33

Billy Martin, the longtime if irregularly appointed Yankee manager, in one of his most famous moments—kicking dirt all over umpire Dallas Parks in a 1979 game against Minnesota.

promptly bringing New York three straight pennants. The loquacious Martin argued with Reggie Jackson constantly and at one point in 1978 told reporters that both Jackson and Steinbrenner were liars. He was fired. Then he was back. Then he punched a marshmallow salesman and was fired again. Then he was hired by Oakland and two years later he was fired again. Then it was back to New York to be hired and fired several more times. Altogether, Martin managed the Yankees five different times in the '80s.

1983: Billy teeters with Yogi in the wings, and 1985: Yogi's down, Billy's back.

Kids' favorite players

Don Mattingly. He can hit for a .300 average and he can hit for power. I love the way he hits, the way he tries so hard. And I admire him for working as hard as he does at hitting, like he can always improve. Few players are like that.

—Mike Aiello, 13

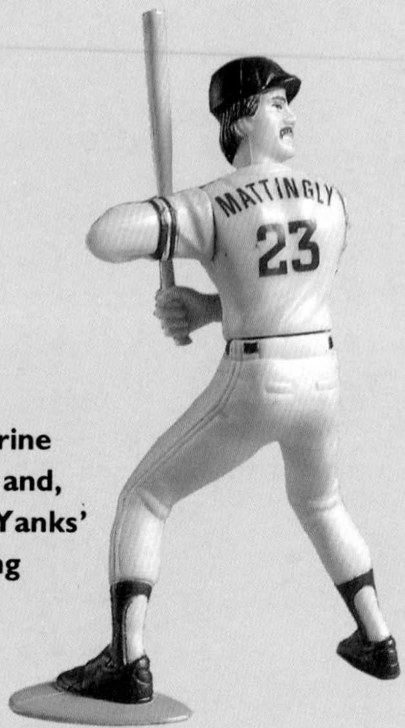

Mattingly figurine from the '80s, and, opposite, the Yanks' galaxy of young stars.

Kevin Maas, one of the promising young Yankees.

Kevin Maas. I like that weird stance of his. He is a very strong player and can hit one out at any time. He's a dangerous hitter, someone who can produce in any inning, in any situation.

—Rocky Flores, 17

Rickey Henderson. When he was with the Yanks, you'd know he'd steal second or third whenever he wanted to. It was exciting just to watch him take that lead off first, daring the pitcher. And when he'd go, whoa! The whole place would be on their feet, just to see if he'd beat the throw. The guy was electric.

—Jason Tarsi, 14

GALAXY OF
YOUNG STARS

The night before I arrived at Yankee Stadium for the first time I was lying in bed in my hotel room. I couldn't think of anything except going into the Yankee manager's office the next day. Bucky Harris. Miller Huggins. Casey Stengel. Billy Martin. Ralph Houk. So many legends of the game were Yankee managers. I got goose bumps when I walked in. I could kinda, kinda feel them there. . . .

—1990–91 Yankee Manager STUMP MERRILL

In the spring of 1990 the Steinbrenner years at Yankee Stadium ended with shock when the Boss was forced to relinquish leadership of the team following an investigation into his ties to a New York gambler. A long and colorful era came to an abrupt end. But even as Steinbrenner was preparing to leave Yankee Stadium, a new era was beginning for the Bronx Bombers. There was a new manager, Stump Merrill, a portly, rugged, tobacco-chomping skipper from the old school, superstar Don Mattingly, and a whole new youth corps of remarkable talent—talent that could bring the Yankees back to glory in the '90s.

Mattingly is, without question, the new pride of the Yankees. He came up in 1984 and became an immediate star. The team captain has averaged over .320 at the plate with twenty-five to thirty home runs and one hundred RBIs per year, and has given the team power and clutch hitting. The first to arrive at the ballpark and often the last to leave, Mattingly, like Ted Williams, spends most of his waking moments trying to improve his game.

"I admire Don Mattingly more than any other active ballplayer," says retired Dodger great Duke Snider. "He works very, very hard for what he has. I think that if kids want to look up to somebody,

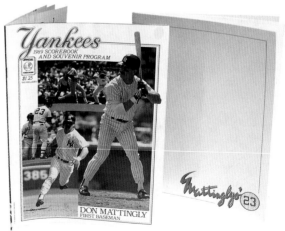

they should look up to a guy like Mattingly who works so hard on the field and who is a good, clean-living family man off it."

But Mattingly is no one-man team. The "new" Yankees, the youth corps, is full of power. Kevin Maas, brought up in the middle of 1990, stunned baseball by becoming a home-run sensation. Hensley Meulens, Bernie Williams, and a number of

Above, first baseman Don Mattingly is widely regarded as one of the hardest working athletes in baseball; above right, his American League MVP patch from 1985.

Right, Mattingly graces a 1989 Yankee program cover next to a menu from his Indiana restaurant (where dozens of Yankee fans fly for New Year's Eve).

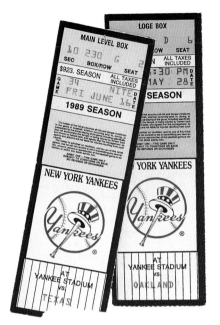

Stubs from '89 and '61.

other rookies brought up last year joined Roberto Kelly, Mel Hall, Steve Sax, and Jesse Barfield to create a potentially deadly young lineup. Scott Kamieniecki, Scott Sanderson, Wade Taylor, and Steve Howe make up a tough young pitching staff. The team, still growing, could evolve into a powerhouse once again.

Like generations before them, the real Yankee fans never left the team when they began their seemingly endless slump in 1982. Even though today's fans are not

A Yankee clock.

Don Mattingly is the hardest working ballplayer in the game. He spends a half hour each day just hitting balls off a kids' batting tee. He takes indoor batting practice and outdoor batting practice. He treats batting practice like the seventh game of the World Series. He is as good as he is because he works hard at it. A guy like that is always going to come through for you in tight situations because he's trained to do it. There's no luck involved with guys like that—they're trained, they're ready, and in critical situations they will always produce.

—DARRELL EVANS, Detroit Tigers All Star

119

YANKEE FANS

The Hartland Statue Company made Mantle, Ruth, and Berra figures in the '60s as part of its Hartland Heroes series.

A World Series pin—the Yankees again.

I remember my first game. My dad got me three hot dogs. Three! And I had a big soda. And the other kid and his father who were going to meet us were real late because of the traffic.

—DAVID BENNETT, 5, of Long Island

Yankees banners, including the lower one from the 1958 Series.

I brought my five-year-old here for the first time a few weeks ago and I think I wound up buying him everything for sale at the souvenir counter. The first game I ever saw here was with my dad and now I'm here with David. It's nice, coming to the game that way, the way my dad did with me.

—RICH BENNETT, 36, of Long Island

The Yankee fans hate to lose. If the team wins two straight, the fans will buy half the stuff at my stand on the way out. If the team loses two straight, the fans will march right past me, not stopping, with scowls on their faces. My sales are in direct proportion to the American League standings.

—ETON REID, Yankee Stadium souvenir salesman

These 1950s playing cards featured a kid swinging a bat while Ruth looked down from heaven.

A brilliant picture of the Babe dedicated "To my pal Jimmie Thompson, a power- ful 'man,' Sincerely 'Babe' Ruth."

I started a scrapbook when I was eight years old. It was this big, thick old business ledger. I would cut articles and pictures out of newspapers. I cut the cor- ners off the pictures so the page numbers of the book would show. I kept the book all my life and later, when my brother and I had a store, I got any sports figures who came in, like Tommy Henrich, to sign it for me. When I look at it now, late at night, I feel like I'm eight again.

—TONY MARCELLO of Boonton, New Jersey

always wanted to play center field for the Yankees. I never realized what a big thing it was with fans until I got here. People keep telling me about the center fielders here, like DiMaggio and Mantle, and how they covered all that ground out there. I cover it well, too, but I know they played when center field was about sixty feet deeper and you had the flagpole and monuments. I know how hard it is to cover that ground now, so I really admire DiMaggio and Mantle for covering so much more ground with what always appeared to be so little effort. A player never appreciates a great center fielder until he goes out there and tries to do it himself where they did it. They were great.

—ROBERTO KELLY, New York Yankees

This All-Star ring belonged to a Yankee executive; opposite, the Bombers forever: more Yankees memorabilia.

particularly crazy about the renovation of Yankee Stadium done in 1973, which brought the end of the gloried rooftop facade and the center-field monuments, they have supported the team through the last quarter century. They've bought more Yankee souvenirs, memorabilia, and baseball cards during the '80s, for instance, than any other team's fans, and Yankee attendance has remained consistently among the best of all major league clubs.

Why haven't the Yankees continued to dominate? Was it the ridiculous hirings and firings of so many managers and the lack of stability in the dugout under Steinbrenner? Was it a mediocre minor-league system? Is it the thin pitching, year after year? Are the other ball clubs in the division and league, like the rejuvenated Orioles, the streaking Blue Jays, and the always tough Red Sox, really that good?

No one is certain, but today's fans continue to worship their team, because they know that if the Yankees can just develop their young pitchers, and the hitting can stay strong into August, and if a few more rookies could come up. . . .

There's no place like New York in October, and no place like Yankee Stadium, with all those glorious pinstriped ghosts patrolling the field.

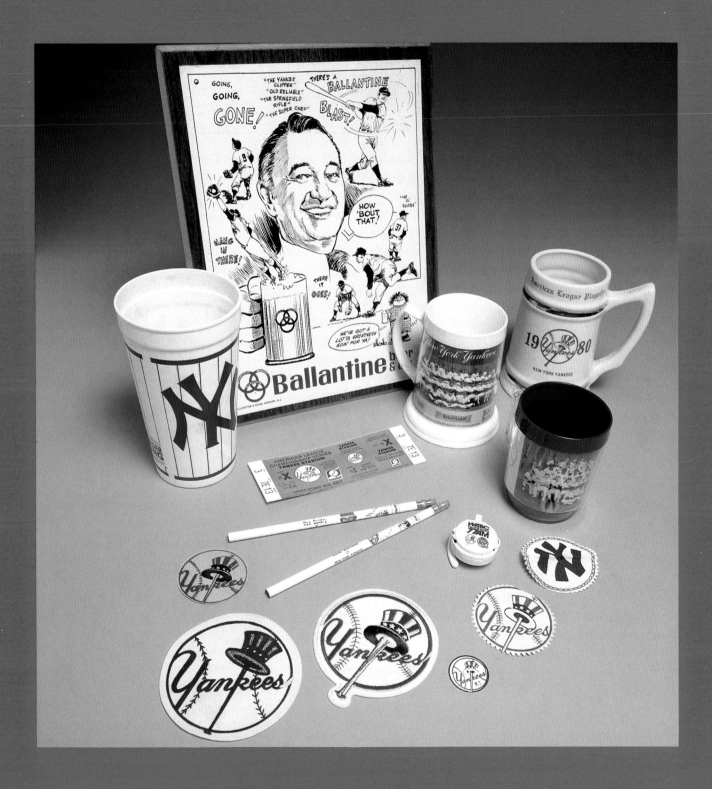

YANKEE GREATS

YOGI BERRA coach

YOGI BERRA

In his years as player, manager, and coach, the great Yankee catcher of the '50s became more than just a star. His cockeyed sayings became part of the American language, from the immortal remark "It ain't over till it's over" to such inspired observations as "Nobody goes to that restaurant anymore, it's too crowded."

But Berra the philosopher would never have been the Will Rogers of the ballpark if he hadn't produced in the lineup—and he produced. He led the league in games caught eight times and in double plays six times, and he had an uncanny ability to size up his pitchers each day.

Yogi was also a dangerous slugger who hit thirty home runs during two seasons, and 306 lifetime while posting five 100-RBI seasons. A seasoned hitter with a good eye, he rarely struck out and became a noted clutch hitter, hitting .285 lifetime and playing in fourteen World Series. Berra was inducted into the Hall of Fame in 1972.

JOE DiMAGGIO

The fabled Yankee Clipper is best known for hitting safely in fifty-six consecutive games in 1941, but his career stats are mind-boggling. DiMaggio hit .325 lifetime with 361 home runs and 1,537 RBIs. He was named MVP three times. And he accomplished all of this while taking three years out of his career to serve in the military during World War II.

DiMaggio was a splendid outfielder who always had the jump on the ball. "You don't go when you hear the crack of the bat—you go before you hear it," he said.

As a Yankee for fifteen years, Joe was a quiet but stern leader who took the team to eight World Series, including one in his very

JOE DiMAGGIO
OUTFIELDER

first year. He was also a folk hero, heralded in 1940s songs like "Joltin' Joe DiMaggio" and the 1969 hit "Mrs. Robinson." He was inducted into the Hall of Fame in 1955.

WHITEY FORD

Ford was the Yankees' "money" pitcher in the heyday of the '50s. It was always Whitey who won the close ones, Whitey who enabled the Bronx Bombers to win the pennants, always Whitey winning the World Series big ones. And it was Whitey, the soft-spoken, easy-smiling pitcher, who finally broke Babe Ruth's record of scoreless innings in World Series play.

As a rookie Ford was a sensation right away, coming up to the Yankees mid-season in 1950 and winning his first nine games. He spent the next two years in the service, then returned with an impressive 18–6 record. Lifetime, he posted a 236–106 mark with a winning percentage of .690. But his most remarkable statistic is that in eleven of sixteen seasons his ERA was under 3.00. Ford was inducted into the Hall of Fame in 1974.

LOU GEHRIG

BIG LEAGUE CHEWING GUM

LOU GEHRIG

The Iron Horse played in a record 2,130 games but he always lived in the shadow of Ruth. Indeed if there had been no Ruth, Gehrig would certainly have been the dominant player in the '20s and '30s. He ripped 493 home runs, drove in 1,990 runs, and batted .340 during a remarkable career that ended only when a soon-to-be fatal illness forced him to leave the game in 1939.

Gehrig was a bulky, strong first baseman and an effective clutch hitter who could hit with devastating power to all fields. Few remember that the year Ruth hit sixty home runs, Gehrig hit forty-seven, and on September 1 of that year he had led Ruth, forty-six to forty-five.

LEFTY GOMEZ

The brilliant left-handed pitcher from the 1930s, who teamed with Red Ruffing for a lethal one-two punch on the mound, was one of the game's most colorful characters. Forever cracking jokes or halting a game to stare at airplanes flying overhead, Lefty would leave players, teammates, and opponents with smiles on their faces.

Before he died in 1990, Lefty became a frequent guest signer at baseball card shows. One of his favorite tricks was to take a baseball someone wanted him to sign, turn to another player signing autographs ten feet away, yell, and throw the ball at him. The other player would miss it, of course, and Gomez would bellow, "Good God, forty years later and you still can't catch!"

Gomez, who entered the Hall of Fame in 1972, won twenty-one games in his third season with the Yankees, twenty-six in 1934, and went on to post a 189–102 lifetime record with a matchless 6–0 record in World Series play.

REGGIE JACKSON

The flamboyant, controversial Jackson created a stir wherever he went, and during his five years with the Yankees he claimed the prime time of the media spotlight. Reggie was fabled for outspoken remarks ("I'm the straw that stirs the drink") and for arguments with manager Billy Martin, but he backed up everything with his bat. Known as "Mr. October" for his World Series heroics, he became a star with every team he joined (he played for the Yanks, A's, Angels, and Orioles). During his twenty-one-year career he hit 563 home runs and batted in 1,702 runs.

Yankees REGGIE JACKSON of

Reggie played with eleven divisional winners, six pennant winners, five world champions, and he had a lifetime .357 average in the World Series. But his finest moment came in the deciding, sixth game of the '77 Series against the Dodgers, when he hit three consecutive home runs, each on the first pitch he was thrown.

No one enjoyed his achievements more than he did. Just as impressive as his home runs was the way he'd stand at home plate and admire them as they flew over the fence. Indeed Jackson once remarked that he didn't like watching the World Series on television "because I couldn't see myself play."

535 REGINALD MARTINEZ JACKSON

Born: May 18, 1946   Home: Oakland, Calif.
Ht.: 6'0"   Wgt.: 206   Bats: Left   Throws: Left   ©1982 DONRUSS

RECENT MAJOR LEAGUE PERFORMANCE

Year	Team Name	Bat. Avg.	Games	At Bat	Hits	Runs	2B	3B	HR	RBI	Steal	Walk	SO
1977	Yankees	.286	146	525	150	93	39	2	32	110	17	75	129
1978	Yankees	.274	139	511	140	82	13	5	27	97	14	58	133
1979	Yankees	.297	131	465	138	78	24	2	29	89	9	65	107
1980	Yankees	.300	143	514	154	94	22	4	41	111	1	83	122
1981	Yankees	.237	94	334	79	33	17	1	15	54	0	46	82
Career		.271	2018	7197	1953	1178	362	42	425	1285	212	981	1810

CAREER HIGHLIGHTS

Became a free agent for the second time after last season...First free agency was '76 when he left Baltimore and signed with Yankees...Is 18th on the all-time HR list... Despite subpar '81 season, still led Yanks in HR...Hero of '77 and '78 World Series for Yanks when he hit .450 and .391 respectively and 8 RBI in each...Hit 4 straight HR in '77 Series...Named AL MVP in '73 with A's when he hit .293 and led league in HR (32) and RBI (117).

KEELER, N.Y. AMER.

WEE WILLIE KEELER

Keeler was one of the original New York Highlanders, coming to New York after prosperous years in Baltimore and Brooklyn. His .345 lifetime average is one of the highest in history and in 1897 with Baltimore he hit .432. The 5 feet, 5 inch Keeler was more than just a good hitter, though, and his oft-quoted line, "hit 'em where they ain't," was remembered for good reason. He was a superb bunter and a precise place hitter who could drop a soft liner over any second baseman's head to drive in a run. He originated the "Baltimore chop," the downward swing that caused a high bouncer, which could be beat out to first.

Wee Willie played with New York longer than with any other team and his annual .300-plus batting averages established the franchise in the fledgling American League. He went to Cooperstown in 1939.

MICKEY MANTLE
OUTFIELDER

MICKEY MANTLE

Of all the legends that grew up around Mickey Mantle, perhaps the most remarkable concerned his rookie speed—before he tore his knee in his first season, Mantle was one of the fastest runners in baseball.

It was at the plate, though, that Number Seven was ferocious. Lifetime he hit .298, hammered 536 home runs, recorded 1,509 RBIs, and still holds the record for home runs in the World Series with eighteen. Mantle's home runs were titanic. He came closer than anyone has to hitting a home run out of Yankee Stadium, and did hit homers out of other stadiums, the longest being the 565-foot shot out of Griffith Stadium in Washington, D.C.

After all that, when pressed the Mick says that one of the things he is proudest of is the little-known fact that he played 2,401 games. The Cooperstown doors swung open for Mickey in 1974 with best buddy Whitey Ford.

DON MATTINGLY

The current star of the Yankees and the squad's captain, Mattingly has pledged himself to take the team to the World Series. In the early '80s he quickly established himself as one of the game's top players with a string of .300-plus seasons topped with a sterling .343 in 1984 that won the batting championship. He once hit six grand slams in one year, smacked two hundred hits three seasons in a row, and hit eight home runs in eight straight games.

His hard work and dedication have made Mattingly a favorite among teammates and fans. He works himself mercilessly during the season and in the off season to hone his odd, high-handed, backward-leaning swing. He is also a player who has surprised his toughest critics with his amazing ability to begin many seasons hitting close to .200 and finishing over .300.

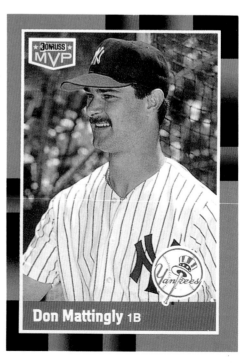

Don Mattingly 1B

PHIL RIZZUTO
SHORTSTOP-NEW YORK YANKEES

PHIL RIZZUTO

The Scooter is perhaps the best player in baseball history not to have made the Hall of Fame. Rizzuto, a fine shortstop and a superb bunter, hit .273 lifetime with 562 RBIs, won the MVP award in 1950, and played on three All-Star teams. In addition to having played in nine World Series, he stands seventh in World Series hits with forty-five and third in steals with ten.

After retiring from the Yankees in 1956, Rizzuto went on to a long career as a Yankee broadcaster, where he made the expression "holy cow" a household word. He also became famous for announcing the birthdays of thousands of people on the air and for his good-natured banter with longtime on-air colleague and later National League president Bill White.

BABE RUTH

Between his hitting, his pitching, and his carousing, it would take an entire book to list the accomplishments of Babe Ruth. Ruth was the first man to hit twenty-nine home runs in a season, the first to hit fifty, and the first to hit sixty. His 714 career home runs established a record for forty years. In addition he hit a remarkable .342 lifetime with 2,204 RBIs. But the Babe was even a better pitcher than a hitter, compiling a sparkling 94–46 record on the mound, including a remarkable 1916 season with Boston when he went 23–12 with an astonishing 1.75 ERA.

Ruth was such a beloved figure that an entire stadium had to be built to hold the hordes of people who flocked to Yankees games to see him. The Hall-of-Famer led the team as it became the first great dynasty in American sport, and as a player and a personality he dominated his time like no other man or woman before or since.

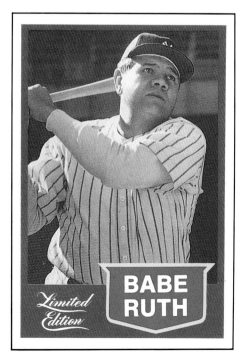

Limited Edition

BABE RUTH

YANKEE STATS

ALL-TIME YANKEES—TOP 20 PITCHING CATEGORIES

GAMES		WINS		STRIKEOUTS		COMPLETE GAMES	
Righetti	522	Ford, W.	236	Ford, W.	1956	Ruffing	261
Ford, W.	498	Ruffing	231	Guidry	1778	Gomez	173
Ruffing	426	Gomez	189	Ruffing	1526	Chesbro	169
Lyle	420	Guidry	170	Gomez	1468	Pennock	165
Shawkey	415	Shawkey	168	Stottlemyre	1257	Shawkey	161
Murphy	383	Stottlemyre	164	Shawkey	1163	Ford, W.	156
Guidry	368	Pennock	162	Downing	1028	Hoyt	156
Gomez	367	Hoyt	157	Reynolds	967	Stottlemyre	152
Hoyt	365	Reynolds	131	Righetti	940	Caldwell	151
Stottlemyre	360	Chesbro	126	Chesbro	913	Chandler	109
Pennock	346	Raschi	120	Turley	909	Warhop	105
Hamilton	331	Lopat	113	Peterson	893	Ford, R.	103
Gossage	319	Peterson	109	Raschi	832	Orth	102
Reynolds	295	Chandler	109	Caldwell	803	Raschi	99
Peterson	288	Caldwell	96	Hoyt	713	Reynolds	96
Page	278	Murphy	93	Pennock	656	Guidry	95
Chesbro	269	Pipgras	93	Pipgras	652	Bonham	91
Caldwell	248	John	91	Terry	615	Lopat	91
Pipgras	247	Turley	82	Chandler	614	Pipgras	84
Reniff	247	Mays	79	Byrne	592	Quinn	82
		Bonham	79				

INNINGS		PCT. (100 Decis.)		ERA (Over 800 Inn.)		SHUTOUTS	
Ford, W.	3171	Chandler	.717	Ford, R.	2.54	Ford, W.	45
Ruffing	3169	Raschi	.706	Chesbro	2.58	Stottlemyre	40
Stottlemyre	2662	Ford, W.	.690	Orth	2.72	Ruffing	40
Gomez	2498	Reynolds	.686	Bonham	2.73	Gomez	28
Shawkey	2489	Mays	.670	Ford, W.	2.74	Reynolds	27
Guidry	2392	Lopat	.657	Chandler	2.84	Chandler	26
Hoyt	2273	Gomez	.652	Fisher	2.91	Guidry	26
Pennock	2190	Guidry	.651	Stottlemyre	2.97	Shawkey	24
Chesbro	1953	Ruffing	.651	Caldwell	2.99	Raschi	24
Peterson	1856	Pennock	.643	Warhop	3.09	Turley	21
Caldwell	1718	Byrne	.643	Peterson	3.10	Lopat	20
Reynolds	1700	Murphy	.637	Shawkey	3.10	Pennock	19
Raschi	1537	Hoyt	.616	Bahnsen	3.10	Peterson	18
Lopat	1497	Bonham	.612	Righetti	3.11	Bonham	17
Chandler	1485	Turley	.612	Quinn	3.12	Chesbro	16
Warhop	1423	John	.603	Lopat	3.25	Terry	16
Fisher	1380	Pipgras	.595	Downing	3.25	Hoyt	15
John	1366	Chesbro	.577	Mays	3.25	Pipgras	13
Pipgras	1352	Terry	.569	Guidry	3.29	Caldwell	13
Quinn	1279	Righetti	.548	Reynolds	3.30	Downing	12
						John	12

ALL-TIME YANKEES—TOP 20 BATTING CATEGORIES

GAMES

Mantle	2401
Gehrig	2164
Berra	2116
Ruth	2084
White	1881
Dickey	1789
DiMaggio	1736
Randolph	1694
Crosetti	1682
Rizzuto	1661
Lazzeri	1659
Nettles	1535
Howard	1492
Pipp	1488
Combs	1455
Munson	1423
Richardson	1412
Bauer	1406
McDougald	1323
Meusel	1294

RUNS

Ruth	1959
Gehrig	1888
Mantle	1677
DiMaggio	1390
Combs	1186
Berra	1174
Randolph	1027
Crosetti	1006
White	964
Lazzeri	952
Rolfe	942
Dickey	930
Henrich	901
Rizzuto	877
Pipp	820
Bauer	792
Meusel	764
Nettles	750
Winfield	722
Keller	714

DOUBLES

Gehrig	535
Ruth	424
DiMaggio	389
Mantle	344
Dickey	343
Meusel	338
Lazzeri	327
Berra	321
Combs	309
White	300
Mattingly	288
Henrich	269
Crosetti	260
Randolph	259
Pipp	259
Rolfe	257
Rizzuto	239
Winfield	236
Munson	229
Howard	211

HOME RUNS

Ruth	659
Mantle	536
Gehrig	493
DiMaggio	361
Berra	358
Nettles	250
Winfield	205
Maris	203
Dickey	202
Keller	184
Henrich	183
Murcer	175
Lazzeri	169
Mattingly	169
Pepitone	166
Skowron	165
Howard	161
White	160
Bauer	158
Gordon	153

AT BATS

Mantle	8102
Gehrig	8001
Berra	7546
Ruth	7217
DiMaggio	6821
White	6550
Randolph	6303
Dickey	6300
Crosetti	6277
Lazzeri	6094
Rizzuto	5816
Combs	5748
Pipp	5594
Nettles	5519
Richardson	5386
Munson	5344
Howard	5044
Meusel	5032
Rolfe	4827
Bauer	4784

HITS

Gehrig	2721
Ruth	2518
Mantle	2415
DiMaggio	2214
Berra	2148
Dickey	1969
Combs	1866
White	1803
Lazzeri	1784
Randolph	1731
Rizzuto	1588
Pipp	1577
Meusel	1565
Munson	1558
Crosetti	1541
Richardson	1432
Howard	1405
Mattingly	1401
Nettles	1396
Rolfe	1394

TRIPLES

Gehrig	162
Combs	154
DiMaggio	131
Pipp	121
Lazzeri	115
Ruth	106
Meusel	87
Henrich	73
Mantle	72
Dickey	72
Keller	69
Rolfe	67
Stirnweiss	66
Crosetti	65
Chapman	64
Rizzuto	62
Cree	62
Conroy	59
Randolph	58
Bauer	56

RUNS BATTED IN

Gehrig	1991
Ruth	1970
DiMaggio	1537
Mantle	1509
Berra	1430
Dickey	1209
Lazzeri	1154
Meusel	1005
Nettles	834
Pipp	825
Winfield	818
Henrich	795
Mattingly	759
White	758
Howard	732
Keller	723
Munson	701
Murcer	687
Skowron	672
Bauer	654

BATTING AVG. (500 or more games)

Ruth	.349	Piniella	.295
Gehrig	.340	Skowron	.294
Combs	.325	Keeler	.294
DiMaggio	.325	Peckinpaugh	.294
Mattingly	.317	Lazzeri	.293
Dickey	.312	Cree	.292
Meusel	.311	Munson	.292
Chapman	.305	Selkirk	.290
Mantle	.298	Winfield	.290
Schang	.297	Rolfe	.289

STOLEN BASES

Henderson	326	Lazzeri	147
Randolph	251	Daniels	145
Chase	248	Peckinpaugh	143
White	233	Cree	132
Chapman	184	Meusel	131
Conroy	184	Stirnweiss	130
Maisel	183	Keeler	118
Mantle	153	Pipp	114
Clarke	151	Crosetti	113
Rizzuto	149	Ruth	110

131

ALL-TIME YANKEE PITCHING RECORDS INDIVIDUAL

Most years with Yankees . . . . Whitey Ford 16 (1950, 53–67)

Most games, right-hander, season . . . . Pedro Ramos 65 (1965)

Dooley Womack 65 (1967)

Most games, left-hander, season . . . . Dave Righetti 74 (1985)

Dave Righetti 74 (1986)

Most games started, season . . . . Jack Chesbro 51 (1904)

Most complete games, season . . . . Jack Chesbro 48 (1904)

Most innings pitched, season . . . . Jack Chesbro 454 (1904)

Most victories, RHP, season . . . . Jack Chesbro 41 (1904)

Most victories, LHP, season . . . . Lefty Gomez 26 (1934)

Most 20-victory seasons . . . . Bob Shawkey 4

Lefty Gomez 4

Red Ruffing 4

Most losses, season . . . . Al Orth 21 (1907)

Sam Jones 21 (1925)

Joe Lake 21 (1908)

Russ Ford 21 (1912)

Highest winning percentage, season . . . . Ron Guidry (25–3) 893 (1978)

Most consecutive victories, season . . . . Jack Chesbro 14 (1904)

Whitey Ford 14 (1961)

Most consecutive losses, season . . . . William Hogg 9 (1908)

Thad Tillotson 9 (1967)

Most saves, left-hander, season . . . . Dave Righetti 46 (1986)

Most saves, right-hander, season . . . . Rich Gossage 33 (1980)

Most walks, left-hander, season . . . . Tommy Byrne 179 (1949)

Most walks, right-hander, season . . . . Bob Turley 177 (1955)

Most strikeouts, season . . . . Ron Guidry 248 (1978)

Most strikeouts, 9-inning game . . . . Ron Guidry 18 (6/17/78)

Most strikeouts, extra-inning game . . . . Whitey Ford 15 (4/22/59)

Most shutouts, season . . . . Ron Guidry 9 (1978)

Most shutouts lost, season . . . . Bill Zuber 7 (1945)

Most runs allowed, season . . . . Russ Ford 165 (1912)

Most earned runs allowed, season . . . . Sam Jones 127 (1925)

Most hits allowed, season . . . . Jack Chesbro 337 (1904)

Most hit batsmen, season . . . . John Warhop 26 (1909)

Most wild pitches, season . . . . Al Downing 14 (1964)

Most home runs allowed, season . . . . Ralph Terry 40 (1962)

Lowest E.R.A., season, right-handed . . . . Spud Chandler 1.64 (1943)

Lowest E.R.A., season, left-handed . . . . Ron Guidry 1.74 (1978)

All-Time Yankee Batting Records Individual

Most years with Yankees	Yoga Berra	18 (1946–63)
	Mickey Mantle	(1951–68)
Most games, season	Bobby Richardson	162 (1961)
	Roy White	162 (1970)
	Chris Chambliss	162 (1978)
	Don Mattingly	162 (1986)
	Roberto Kelly	162 (1990)
Most at bats, season	Bobby Richardson	692 (1962)
Most runs, season	Babe Ruth	177 (1921)
Most hits, season	Don Mattingly	238 (1986)
Most singles, season	Steve Sax	171 (1989)
Most doubles, season	Don Mattingly	53 (1986)
Most triples, season	Earle Combs	23 (1927)
Most home runs, right-hander, season	Joe DiMaggio	46 (1937)
Most home runs, left-hander, season	Roger Maris	61 (1961)
Most home runs, rookie, season	Joe DiMaggio	29 (1936)
Most grand slam home runs, season	Don Mattingly	6 (1987)
Most grand slam home runs, career	Lou Gehrig	23
Most home runs, season, at home	Babe Ruth	32 (1921)
	Lou Gehrig	30 (1934)
	Roger Maris	30 (1961)
Most home runs, season, on the road	Babe Ruth	32 (1927)
Most total bases, season	Babe Ruth	457 (1921)
Most sacrifice hits, season	Willie Keeler	42 (1905)
Most sacrifice flies, season	Roy White	17 (1971)
Most stolen bases, season	Rickey Henderson	93 (1988)
Most caught stealing, season	Ben Chapman	23 (1931)
Most walks, season	Babe Ruth	170 (1923)
Most strikeouts, season	Jack Clark	141 (1988)
Fewest strikeouts, season	Joe Sewell	3 (1932)
Most hit by pitch, season	Don Baylor	24 (1985)
Most runs batted in, season	Lou Gehrig	184 (1931)
Most consecutive games with a home run	Don Mattingly	8 (1987)
Highest batting average, season	Babe Ruth	.393 (1923)
Highest slugging average, season	Babe Ruth	.847 (1920)
Longest hitting streak	Joe DiMaggio	56 (1941)
Most grounded into double plays, season	Dave Winfield	30 (1983)
Fewest grounded into double plays, season	Mickey Mantle	2 (1961)
	Mickey Rivers	2 (1977)

AUTOGRAPH PAGES

BIBLIOGRAPHY

Allen, Maury. *Where Have You Gone, Joe DiMaggio?* New York: E. P. Dutton, 1975.

————. *Damned Yankee: The Billy Martin Story.* New York: Times Books, 1986.

Berra, Yogi, with Tom Horton. *Yogi: It Ain't Over.* New York: McGraw-Hill, 1989.

Forker, Dom. *The Men of Autumn.* Dallas: Taylor Publishing, 1989.

————. *Sweet Seasons: Recollections of the 1955–64 New York Yankees.* Dallas: Taylor Publishing, 1990.

Frommer, Harvey. *Baseball's Greatest Rivalry: The New York Yankees vs. the Boston Red Sox.* New York: Atheneum Publishers, 1982.

Golenbock, Peter. *Dynasty: The New York Yankees, 1949–1964.* New York: Berkley Books, 1975.

Halberstam, David. *The Summer of '49.* New York: William Morrow, 1989.

Honig, Donald. *The New York Yankees: An Illustrated History.* New York: Crown Publishers, 1987.

Lally, Dick. *Pinstripe Summer: Memories of Yankee Seasons Past.* New York: Arbor House, 1985.

Linn, Ed. *Steinbrenner's Yankees.* New York: Holt, Rinehart & Winston, 1982.

Lyle, Sparky, and Peter Golenbock. *The Bronx Zoo.* New York: Crown Publishers, 1979.

Madden, Bill, and Moss Klein. *Damned Yankees.* New York: Warner Books, 1990.

Mantle, Mickey. *The Education of a Baseball Player.* New York: Simon and Schuster, 1967.

Mantle, Mickey, and Herb Gluck. *The Mick.* New York: Doubleday, 1985.

Meany, Tom. *The Yankee Story.* New York: E. P. Dutton, 1960.

Mosedale, John. *The Greatest of All—The 1927 New York Yankees.* New York: Dial Press, 1974.

Ruth, Babe, and Bob Considine. *The Babe Ruth Story.* New York: E. P. Dutton, 1948.

Seidel, Michael. *Joe DiMaggio and the Summer of '41.* New York: Penguin, 1989.

Tullius, John. *I'd Rather Be a Yankee.* New York: Jove Books, 1986.

INDEX

A

Abbott, Jim, quoted, 57
Allen, Mel, quoted, 46, 50
All-Star ring, 122
Amoros, Sandy, 72

B

Babe Ruth Award, Whitey
　Ford's, 82
Babe Ruth Boys Club, pin, 25
Baker, Frank "Home Run,"
　19–20
balls, 36, 77; Joe DiMaggio, 13,
　52; Whitey Ford, 82;
　Thurman Munson, 106; Babe
　Ruth, 26, 27
banners: 60; Mickey Mantle
　Day, 54; World Series, 1958,
　120
Barfield, Jesse, 119
Barrow, Ed, 28
baseball cards: Joe DiMaggio,
　52, 53; Don Larsen, 74;
　"strip," 35; talking, Mickey
　Mantle, 65
bats, 36, 101; Mickey Mantle,
　89; Thurman Munson, 106;
　Babe Ruth, 26
Bauer, Hank, 60, 66, 79
bean-bag game (Mickey Mantle),
　94
Bench, Johnny, quoted, 103
Berra, Lawrence Peter (Yogi),
　66, 66, 69, 72, 75, 79, 80,
　84, 95, 124, 124; autograph,
　45; commemorative plate,
　66; Hartland Heroes statue,
　120; newspaper feature, 115;
　quoted, 73, 74, 75
Bevens, Floyd, 67–68
board game, Roger Maris, 93
Bodie, Ping, quoted, 24
Bonham, Ernie "Tiny," 57
Boston Red Sox: rivalry with
　New York Yankees, 20, 56,
108–9; Yankee purchases
　from, 28
bottle caps, 69
Boys' Life (magazine), page, 45
Brooklyn Dodgers, 16, 20–21,
　44–45, 67–77
Brown, Bobby, quoted, 80
bubble gum cards, 12
Burke, Mike, 95
Bush, "Bullet" Joe, 28
buttons: 1953 team, 68; 1978
　championship, 109; Thurman
　Munson memorial, 106
Byrne, Tommy, 72

C

Campanella, Roy, 68, 71
caps: Bill Dickey, 44; Thurman
　Munson, 106
Carey, Andy, 79
CBS, 95, 97
Chambliss, Chris, 98
Chance, Frank, 18–19
Chandler, Spud, 46
Charles, Ed, quoted, 63
Chesbro, Jack, 18, 18
Cleveland Indians, 71
clocks, 119; Babe Ruth, 37, 48
Collins, Dave, 111
Collins, Joe, 70, 79, 82
contract, Lou Gehrig, 34
Cooper, Gary, 41
Crosetti, Frank, 43

D

Damn Yankees (play), 63
Dempsey, Jack, 23
Dent, Bucky, 109, 109
Devery, Big Bill, 15, 18, 19
diagram folders, Yankee
　Stadium, 105
Dickey, Bill, 44, 45; autograph,
　45; cap, 44
DiMaggio, Joe, 42, 43, 46, 46–
　57, 52, 60, 124–25, 124;
advertisement for Kraft salad
　dressing, 52; autograph, 52,
　105; balls, 13, 52; baseball
　cards, 52, 53; humidor, 13;
　jersey, 10; "Joltin' Joe
　DiMaggio," 53, 54; license
　plate, 52; magazine features,
　6, 55; memorabilia collection,
　50, 51; quoted, 55
Ditmar, Art, 79
dolls: bobbing head, 65; Babe
　Ruth, 5
Donlin, Mike, 21
Duren, Ryne, glasses of, 95

E

Ebbets Field, World Series,
　1953, 70
Elberfeld, Kid, 18
Esquire (magazine), centerfold
　painting of Yankee Stadium,
　105
Evans, Darrel, quoted, 119
exhibit cards, 84

F

fans: bond with Yankees, 66–
　67; camping out, Yankee
　Stadium, 88; quoted, 27, 53,
　56, 67, 77, 86, 89, 91, 94,
　113, 116, 120–22; with Babe
　Ruth, 25
Farrel, Frank, 15, 18, 19
Feller, Bob, quoted, 104
Figueroa, Ed, 100, 108
figurines, Berra: 120; Mantle,
　120; Mattingly, 116; Ruth,
　120
film posters: *The Pride of the
　Yankees*, 41; *Rawhide*, 34
Finley, Charles, 63
Ford, Whitey, 60, 66, 72, 79–
　80, 82, 84, 89, 125, 125;
　autograph, 82; Babe Ruth
　Award, 82; ball, 82;
memorabilia collection, 81;
　quoted, 84
fotoball, Dave Winfield, 112
Frazee, Harry, 21, 56
Frick, Ford, 90
funeral invitation, Babe Ruth,
　48

G

Gehrig, Lou, 29–34, 29, 30,
　32, 43, 45, 46, 125, 125;
　1927 championship, 38–39;
　contract, 34; disease and
　death, 40–41; farewell
　speech, 31, 40; *The Greatest
　Moments in Sports* (record,
　farewell speech), 31; Knot
　Hole Gang pins, 34;
　memorabilia collection, 33;
　The Pride of the Yankees (film),
　41; *Rawhide* (film) poster, 34;
　and Babe Ruth, contrasted,
　29–31; ticket stubs, Lou
　Gehrig memorial game, 41
Gionfriddo, Al, 68
Gomez, Lefty, 44, 44, 126,
　126; autograph, 47; quoted,
　23
Gorbachev, Mikhail, autograph,
　13
Gordon, Joe, 46
Gossage, Rich "Goose," 98
Greatest Moments in Sports, The
　(record), Lou Gehrig farewell
　speech, 31
Griffey, Ken, 111
Griffith, Clark, 15, 18
Guidry, Ron, 100, 107–8, 107
Gullet, Don, 98, 108

H

Hall, Mel, 119
Harrelson, Bud, quoted, 105
Hartland Heroes statue series
　(Mantle, Berra, Ruth), 120

hats, *36*
Hemingway, Ernest, 54
Henderson, Rickey, 111–12, 116
Henrich, Tommy, 46, *57*
Hilltop Park, 15, *17*; Yankee departure from, 20–21
Hoboken, New Jersey, baseball history in, 15
Home Run Derby, 88–90
Houk, Ralph, 79, 88, 98
Howard, Elston, 66, 79, 80, 82, *84*
Howe, Steve, 119
Hoyt, Waite, 28, 38
Hubbell, Carl, 46
Huggins, Miller, 20, *20*, 28–29
humidor, Joe DiMaggio, *13*
Hunter, Jim "Catfish," 97, *99*
Huston, Tillinghast, 19

J

Jackson, Reggie, 96, 98, 100–102, *102*, 115, 126–27, *126*; autograph, *101*; poster, *101*; quoted, *101*
jerseys: Joe DiMaggio, *10*; Tommy John, *108*; Mickey Mantle, *10*; Johnny Mize, *63*; Thurman Munson, *108*; Babe Ruth, *10*
John, Tommy, *112*, 113; jersey, *108*
"Joltin' Joe DiMaggio," *53*, 54

K

Kamieniecki, Scott, 119
Keane, Johnny, 95
Keeler, Wee Willie, 15, 54–55, *127*, *127*; autograph, *77*; ball, *77*
Keller, Charlie "King Kong," 46
Kelly, Roberto, 119
key chains, Babe Ruth, *26*
Knot Hole Gang (Lou Gehrig's), pins, *34*

Koenig, Mark, 29; quoted, *38*
Kubek, Tony, 79
Kucks, Johnny, 79
Kuzava, Bob, 70

L

Larsen, Don, 73–76, *74*, *76*, 79; baseball card, *74*
Lavagetto, Cookie, 68
Lazzeri, Tony, 29, 38, 43, 46
Lemon, Bob, 109
license plate, Joe DiMaggio, *52*
lighters, *73*; Mickey Mantle, *91*; Babe Ruth, *5*
Lopat, Eddie, 66
Lou Gehrig Day (July 4, 1939), 41
Lou Gehrig Memorial Day (July 4, 1941), 41
Lou Gehrig's Disease, 41
Lyle, Sparky, 100, 108

M

Maas, Kevin, 116, *116*, 118
McCarthy, Joe, 46, *46*
McDougald, Gil, 66, 79; quoted, *67*; Yankee bag, *10*
McGinnity, Joe, 21
McGraw, John, 21
Mack, Connie, 39
MacPhail, Larry, 98
Mantle, Mickey, 54, 60, 69, 72, 78, 88–90, *89*, *90*, 94, 128, *128*; autograph, *77*; ball, *77*; banner, *54*; bat, *89*; bean-bag game, *94*; glove, *91*; Hartland Heroes statue, *120*; jersey, *10*; lighter, *91*; magazine cover story, *65*; memorabilia collection, *86*, *87*; Minute-a-Day Gym, *86*; pin, *90*; quoted, 66, 74, 83, 105; talking baseball card, *65*
Maris, Roger, 88–90, *90*, 92, *92*; board game, *93*;

memorabilia collection, *93*; pin, *90*
Marlzburg, Steve, quoted, 100
Martin, Billy, 70, 71, *71*, 100, 109, 111, 113–15, *114*; newspaper feature, *115*; quoted, 60
Mathewson, Christy, 21
Mattingly, Don, *110*, 111, 116, 117–18, *118*, 128, *128*; figurine, *116*; MVP patch, *118*; restaurant menu, *118*
Mays, Willie, 68
Mazeroski, Bill, 85, *85*
memorabilia. *See individual items, e.g. caps*
memorabilia collections, 4–5, *62*, *123*; Joe DiMaggio, *50*, *51*; Whitey Ford, *81*; Lou Gehrig, *33*; Mickey Mantle, *86*, *87*; Roger Maris, *93*
Merrill, Stump, *117*; quoted, 117
Meulens, Hensley, 118
Meusel, Bob, 29
Mickey Mantle Day, banner, *54*
Minute-a-Day Gym, Mickey Mantle's Isometric, *86*
Mitchell, Dale, 75
Mix, Tom, 27
Mize, Johnny, jersey, *63*
Monroe, Marilyn, 54
Munson, Thurman, 41, 100, 106; autobiography, *106*; autograph, *106*; ball, *106*; bat, *106*; cap, *106*; jersey, *108*; memorial button, *106*
"Murderers Row," 29

N

National League, formation of, 16
Nedick's cup, Roy White, *113*
Nettles, Graig, 98, 100
Newark Bears, 56; books about, 56
Newcombe, Don, 68

New York City: baseball history of, 15–16; dominance of baseball, 44–45
New York Giants, 15, 16, 20–21, 44–45, 46, 68
New York Highlanders, 15–20, *16*
New York Mutuals, 16
New York Yankees: bond with fans, 66–67; early name of (New York Highlanders), 15; fame and greatness of, 11–13; pinstripe uniform, 19; rivalry with Boston Red Sox, 20, 56, 108–9; roots of, 15–21
New York Yankees teams: 1901 team, *14*; 1904–1920 period, 15–21; 1920–1935 period, 23–41; 1927, 39; 1935–1949 period, 43–57; 1949–1960 period, 59–77; 1954 team, *68*; 1960–1973 period, 78–95; 1961 team, *91*; 1973–1978 period, 96–109; 1980–1990 period, 110–22; sketch portrait, *80*; team packet photos, *73*

O

Old Man and the Sea, The (book, Hemingway), 54
Owen, Mickey, 57

P

Parks, Dallas, *114*
Parnell, Mel, 60
patches, Babe Ruth, *37*
Peckinpaugh, Roger, 19
penknife, *108*
Pennock, Herb, 28
Perfect Control (film, Babe Ruth), 37
Philadelphia Athletics, 39
Phil Rizzuto Story (book), 67

Piniella, Lou, 98, 100
pins: Knot Hole Gang, 34; Babe Ruth Boy's Club, 25; Mickey Mantle, 90; Roger Maris, 90; Mother's Day, 95; World Series, 95, 120
pinstripe uniform, 19
Pittsburgh Pirates, 85
plaque, 104
plate (dining), commemorative, 75; Yogi Berra, 66
playing cards, 121
Podres, Johnny, 72
Polo Grounds, Yankees move to, 20–21
posters: Reggie Jackson, 101; The Pride of the Yankees (film), 41; Rawhide (film), 34; World Series, 1927, 38
press pins, World Series, 1927, 25
Pride of the Yankees, The (film), 41; poster, 41
programs, 24; 1950s, 65; 1954, 71; 1960, 63; 1983, 107; 1989, 118; "jay," 65; World Series, 47, 54, 64

R

Ramos, Pedro, quoted, 83
Randolph, Willie, 99; quoted, 98–99
Raschi, Vic, 66
Rawhide (film) poster, 34
Reagan, Ronald, autograph, 13
recording, "Joltin' Joe DiMaggio," 53, 54
"Reggie" (candy bar), 100
restaurant menu, Mattingly, 118
Reynolds, Allie, 66
Richardson, Bobby, 66, 79
Righetti, Dave, commemorative watch, 113
Rivers, Mickey, 100
Rizzuto, Phil, 46, 54, 71, 128, 128; Phil Rizzuto Story (book), 67; quoted, 50
Roaring Twenties, sports during, 23

Robins (Brooklyn Dodgers), 15
Robinson, Bill "Bojangles," 27
Robinson, Jackie, 68, 70
Rockne, Knute, 23
Rolfe, Red, 43, 46
Rose, Howie, quoted, 93
Ruffing, Red, 44
Ruppert, Jacob, 19–21, 19, 28–29
Ruth, George Herman (Babe), 22, 26, 30, 121, 128, 128; autograph, 26, 27; Babe Ruth Boys Club pin, 25; balls, 26, 27; bats, 26; beer advertisement promotion, 27; championship of 1927, 38 –39; chewing tobacco promotion, 21; clocks, 48; departure from Yankees, 43; fans with, 25; farewell to fans, 49; funeral invitation, 48; Lou Gehrig contrasted with, 29–31; Hartland Heroes statue, 120; jersey, 10; key chains, 26; legendary greatness of, 23–28; lighter, 5; patches, 37; Perfect Control (film), 37; pictures of, as decorations on accessories, 26; sale to Yankees, 21; watches, 26; will of, 26

S

Sanderson, Scott, 119
Sax, Steve, 119
schedules, 72
scoreboard T, Yankee Stadium, 104
Selkirk, George, 44
Shantz, Bobby, 79
Sisler, George, 54–55
Skowron, Bill "Moose," 66, 79, 82, 84; quoted, 92
Snider, Duke, 70; autograph, 77; ball, 77; quoted, 76–77, 117–18
Stallings, George, 18

stationery, All-Star, 86
Steinbrenner, George, 97–100, 98, 117; quoted, 111
Stengel, Charles Dillon (Casey), 58, 59–65, 79, 85; magazine cover story, 65
"Subway Series," 44, 45, 67–77

T

Taylor, Wade, 119
telegram, Babe Ruth funeral arrangements, 48
Terry, Ralph, 66, 79, 85, 85; quoted, 92
ticket stubs: 1961, 119; 1989, 119; Lou Gehrig memorial game, 41; World Series, 1928, 55; World Series, 1947, 55; World Series, 1960, 85
Tidrow, Dick, 108
Tilden, Bill, 23
tobacco, chewing (Babe Ruth promotion), 21
Torrez, Mike, 108
Turley, Bob, 66, 72, 79

U

uniform, pinstripe, 19

W

watches: commemorative, 45; Dave Righetti, 113; Babe Ruth, 26
White, Roy, Nedick's cup, 113
Williams, Bernie, 118
Williams, Ted, 56
Winfield, Dave, 111, 112–13; fotoball, 112
Wolverton, Harry, 18
Woodling, Gene, 60
World Series: 1921, 45; 1936,

45–46; banner, 1958, 120; Ebbets Field, 70; 100th Anniversary program, 54; pins, 95, 120; poster, 38; press pin, 25; programs, 47, 54, 64; ticket stub, 1928, 55; ticket stub, 1947, 55; ticket stub, 1960, 85

Y

Yankee haters, 12
Yankee Stadium, 32, 35, 61, 83, 103–5, 103, 104; centerfold painting (Esquire magazine), 105; diagram folders, 105; opening day, 35; renovation, 122; scoreboard T, 104
Yankee Stadium Club: plaque, 104; rules and regulations plaque, 105

139

PHOTOGRAPHY CREDITS

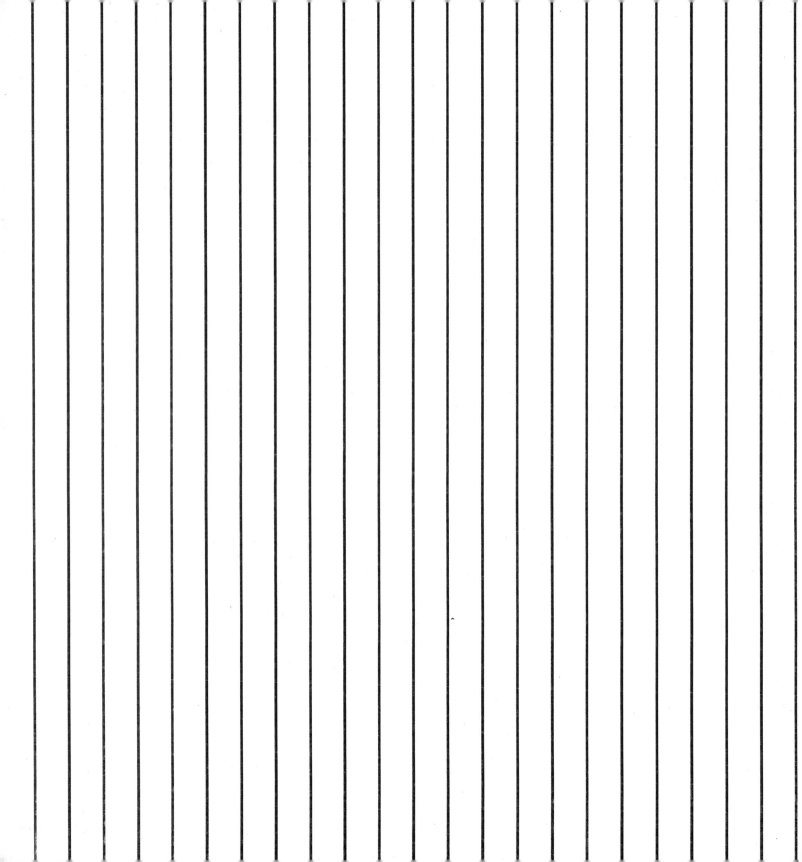